National Curriculum Standards for Social Studies

I Culture

Social studies programs should include experiences that provide for the study of culture and cultural diversity.

II Time, Continuity, & Change

Social studies programs should include experiences that provide for the study of the ways human beings view themselves in and over time while recognizing examples of change and cause and effect relationships.

III People, Places, & Environments

Social studies programs should include experiences that provide for the study of people, places, and environments.

IV Individual Development & Identity

Social studies programs should include experiences that provide for the study of individual development and identity while recognizing personal changes over time and personal connections to places.

V Individuals, Groups, & Institutions

Social studies programs should include experiences that provide for the study of interactions among individuals, groups, and institutions while giving examples of and explaining, group and institutional influences on people, events, and elements of culture.

VI Power, Authority, & Governance

Social studies programs should include experiences that provide for the study of how people create and change structures of power, authority, and governance while examining the rights and responsibilities of the individual in relation to his or her social group.

VII Production, Distribution, & Consumption

Social studies programs should include experiences that provide for the study of how people organize for the production, distribution, and consumption of goods and services.

VIII Science, Technology, & Society

Social studies programs should include experiences that provide for the study of relationships among science, technology, and society.

IX Global Connections

Social studies programs should include experiences that provide for the study of global connections and independence while giving examples of conflict, cooperation, and interdependence among individuals, groups, and nations.

X Civic Ideals & Practices

Social studies programs should include experiences that provide for the study of the ideals, principles, and practices of citizenship in a democratic republic.

National Geography Standards

The *Geographically Informed Person* knows and understands . . .

THE WORLD IN SPATIAL TERMS

STANDARD 1: How to use maps and other geographic representations, tools, and technologies to acquire, process, and report information.

STANDARD 2: How to use mental maps to organize information about people, places, and environments.

STANDARD 3: How to analyze the spatial organization of people, places, and environments on Earth's surface.

PLACES AND REGIONS

STANDARD 4: The physical and human characteristics of places.

STANDARD 5: That people create regions to interpret Earth's complexity.

STANDARD 6: How culture and experience influence people's perception of places and regions.

PHYSICAL SYSTEMS

STANDARD 7: The physical processes that shape the patterns of Earth's surface.

STANDARD 8: The characteristics and spatial distribution of ecosystems on Earth's surface.

HUMAN SYSTEMS

STANDARD 9: The characteristics, distribution, and migration of human populations on Earth's surface.

STANDARD 10: The characteristics, distributions, and complexity of Earth's cultural mosaics.

STANDARD 11: The patterns and networks of economic interdependence on Earth's surface.

STANDARD 12: The process, patterns, and functions of human settlement.

STANDARD 13: How forces of cooperation and conflict among people influence the division and control of Earth's surface.

ENVIRONMENT AND SOCIETY

STANDARD 14: How human actions modify the physical environment.

STANDARD 15: How physical systems affect human systems.

STANDARD 16: The changes that occur in the meaning, use, distribution, and importance of resources.

THE USES OF GEOGRAPHY

STANDARD 17: How to apply geography to interpret the past.

STANDARD 18: To apply geography to interpret the present and plan for the future.

Macmillan/McGraw-Hill TIMELINKS

The World

PROGRAM AUTHORS

James A. Banks
Kevin P. Colleary
Linda Greenow
Walter C. Parker
Emily M. Schell
Dinah Zike

CONTRIBUTORS

Raymond C. Jones
Irma M. Olmedo

 Macmillan/McGraw-Hill

Volume 2

PROGRAM AUTHORS

James A. Banks, Ph.D.
Kerry and Linda Killinger Professor of
   Diversity Studies and Director,
   Center for Multicultural Education
University of Washington
Seattle, Washington

Kevin Colleary, Ed.D.
Curriculum and Teaching Department
Graduate School of Education
Fordham University
New York, New York

Linda Greenow, Ph.D.
Associate Professor and Chair
Department of Geography
State University of New York at
   New Paltz
New Paltz, New York

Walter C. Parker, Ph.D.
Professor of Social Studies Education,
Adjunct Professor of Political Science
University of Washington
Seattle, Washington

Emily M. Schell, Ed.D.
Visiting Professor, Teacher Education
San Diego State University
San Diego, California

Dinah Zike
Educational Consultant
Dinah-Mite Activities, Inc.
San Antonio, Texas

CONTRIBUTORS

Raymond C. Jones, Ph.D.
Director of Secondary Social Studies
   Education
Wake Forest University
Winston-Salem, North Carolina

Irma M. Olmedo
Associate Professor
University of Illinois-Chicago
College of Education
Chicago, Illinois

HISTORIANS/SCHOLARS

Rabbi Pamela Barmash, Ph.D.
Associate Professor of Hebrew Bible
   and Biblical Hebrew and Director,
   Program in Jewish, Islamic and Near
   Eastern Studies
Washington University
St. Louis, Missouri

Thomas Bender, Ph.D.
Professor of History
New York University
New York, New York

Ned Blackhawk
Associate Professor of History and
   American Indian Studies
University of Wisconsin
Madison, Wisconsin

Chun-shu Chang
Department of History
University of Michigan
Ann Arbor, Michigan

Manuel Chavez, Ph.D.
Associate Director, Center for Latin
   American & Caribbean Studies,
   Assistant Professor, School of
   Journalism
Michigan State University
East Lansing, Michigan

Sheilah F. Clarke-Ekong, Ph.D.
Professor of Anthropology
University of Missouri
St. Louis, Missouri

Lawrence Dale, Ph.D.
Director, Center for Economic
   Education
Arkansas State University
Jonesboro, Arkansas

Mac Dixon-Fyle, Ph.D.
Professor of History
DePauw University
Greencastle, Indiana

Carl W. Ernst
William R. Kenan, Jr., Distinguished
   Professor
Department of Religious Studies
Director, Carolina Center for the
   Study of the Middle East and Muslim
   Civilizations
University of North Carolina
Chapel Hill, North Carolina

Brooks Green, Ph.D.
Associate Professor and Chair
Department of Geography
University of Central Arkansas
Conway, Arkansas

The **McGraw·Hill** Companies

 **Macmillan
McGraw-Hill**

Copyright © 2009 by The McGraw-Hill Companies, Inc. All rights reserved. Except as permitted under the United States Copyright Act,
no part of this publication may be reproduced or distributed in any form or by any means, or stored in a database or retrieval system,
without prior permission of the publisher.

Send all inquires to:
Macmillan/McGraw-Hill
8787 Orion Place
Columbus, OH 43240-4027

MHID: 0-02-152406-8
ISBN: 978-0-02-152406-8
Printed in the United States of America.
1 2 3 4 5 6 7 8 9 10   071/043   13 12 11 10 09 08 07

The World
CONTENTS, Volume 2

The Big Idea How do new ideas change people's lives?

Unit 6: A Century of Challenge   273

What causes conflict among people?

Reference Section

Skills and Features, Volume 2

Maps

Cultures and Change

Unit 4

The Big Idea

What makes civilizations change?

FOLDABLES™ **Study Organizer**

Draw Conclusions
Use this top tab book foldable to take notes as you read Unit 4. Your notes will help you answer the Big Idea question. Your foldable's title will be **How Civilizations Change**. Your foldable will have four tabs, labeled **Europe**, **South Asia**, **East Asia**, and **Southeast Asia**.

Europe	South Asia	East Asia	Southeast Asia

LOG ON For more about this unit go to www.macmillanmh.com

Mont St. Michel, Normandy, France

177

PEOPLE, PLACES, and EVENTS

Wu Hou

Charlemagne

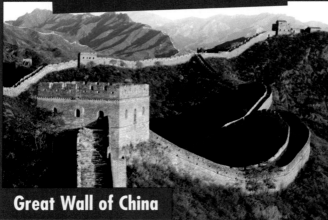

Great Wall of China

690 | Wu Hou rules China as its empress.

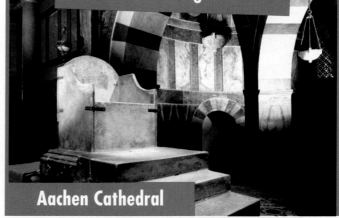

Aachen Cathedral

800 | Charlemagne becomes the Holy Roman Emperor.

650   850   1050

Wu Hou, the only female emperor of China, seized power in 690 and ruled wisely.

Today visitors to China marvel at the **Great Wall of China**, which was expanded in the years after Wu Hou's rule.

After conquering much of western Europe, **Charlemagne** was crowned emperor by Pope Leo III on Christmas Day, 800.

Today you can still see Charlemagne's throne in Aachen, Germany.

LOG ON For more about People, Places, and Events, visit www.macmillanmh.com

Lady Murasaki Shikibu

Shah Jahan

Kyoto Golden Temple

Taj Mahal

c.1000 | Lady Murasaki Shikibu writes *The Tale of Genji*.

1631 | Construction of the Taj Mahal begins.

1250   1450   1650

Lady Murasaki Shikibu wrote one of the world's first novels around 1000.

Today people still read Shikibu's book, *The Tale of Genji*, and visit the Golden Temple in the old Japanese capital, Kyoto, the city where she lived.

When his wife, Mumtaz Mahal, died in 1631, **Shah Jahan** of India built her the spectacular tomb known as the Taj Mahal.

Today people from around the world travel to Agra, India, to see the Taj Mahal.

THE MIDDLE AGES

Lesson 1

VOCABULARY

feudalism p. 182

manor p. 182

vassal p. 182

serf p. 182

guild p. 183

READING SKILL

Draw Conclusions
Use the chart to draw conclusions about daily life for people at different levels of feudal society.

Text Clues	Conclusion

STANDARDS FOCUS

SOCIAL STUDIES — Production, Distribution, and Consumption

GEOGRAPHY — Places and Regions

Charlemagne's troops in battle

Essential Question

How did life change for Europeans during the Middle Ages?

A By the year 800, Charlemagne had reunited much of western Europe.

B When feudalism became a way of life in Europe, everyone in society had a set role.

C Invaders from the north settled in France and conquered England.

180

EUROPE AFTER ROME

To many western Europeans, the fall of the Roman Empire must have seemed like the end of the world. Rome's soldiers had kept the peace for centuries. Now they were gone, and Europe suffered almost constant war. Would anyone be able to take control?

Long after the Roman Empire fell, its culture still connected Europeans—through its roads and aqueducts, and the Latin language. But in most ways, Europe had split apart. No one felt safe or secure. This time was the Middle Ages, the period between the fall of Rome and the 1400s.

Around 790, Charles the Great, also known as Charlemagne became the ruler of a Germanic group called the Franks. Charlemagne's armies conquered territory in today's France, Italy, and Germany.

The Holy Roman Emperor

The early Middle Ages are often called "the Dark Ages" because few Europeans could read or write. Charlemagne built schools and hired judges to write down his laws. He also tried to spread Christianity wherever his troops went.

At Christmas 800, Charlemagne visited Pope Leo III in Rome. As Charlemagne bowed his head to pray, the pope surprised him by placing a gold crown on his head and declaring him emperor. Charlemagne claimed he never expected the crown, but from then on he was the "Holy Roman Emperor." Charlemagne's empire did not last long, though. It split up soon after he died in 814.

QUICK CHECK

Draw Conclusions Why might Charlemagne have pretended to be surprised when he was crowned emperor?

Charlemagne's Empire, A.D. 800

ENGLAND
London
Aachen
Paris
North Sea
ATLANTIC OCEAN
Pyrenees
Alps
Corsica
Sardinia
Adriatic Sea
Rome
Mediterranean Sea
50°N
40°N
10°E
0 100 200 miles
0 100 200 kilometers

Map Skill

LOCATION Which major city was at the southeastern corner of Charlemagne's empire?

▲ In January, nobles celebrate a great feast.

▲ In the spring, serfs plow the manor's farms.

Hand-made, decorated books known as Books of Hours were popular during the Middle Ages.

B LIFE IN THE MIDDLE AGES

In children's stories about the Middle Ages, this period may seem like a time of beautiful castles and brave knights in shining armor. For most Europeans, life during this time was hard and short. Regions suffered terrible periods of war and hunger. Many infants died soon after they were born, and disease killed thousands of people.

Lords and Peasants

The system that helped keep order in Charlemagne's time was **feudalism**. Feudalism worked in different ways in different regions. In many places kings divided their land into **manors**. Manors were large areas of farmland controlled by local leaders called lords. A lord divided control of his land among other nobles called **vassals**. The part of a manor controlled by a vassal was called his fief.

One way a vassal served his lord was by defending the manor as a knight, or armored soldier on horseback. Some knights traveled with their lords to fight in distant lands.

At the bottom of feudal society were the small farmers called **serfs,** or peasants. Serfs farmed a manor's land and, in return, were protected by the lord and his knights. Serfs had few rights. They could not leave their manor or marry each other without their lord's permission. Most serfs shared small huts with their animals outside the walls of the manor's castle. When enemies attacked, the serfs could come inside the castle for protection.

▲ At harvesttime, women collect hay from the fields.

▲ In the winter, serfs still must do their work.

The books included scenes from every month of the year, with prayers for every season.

A Knight's Life

At around age seven, the sons of lords and vassals were sent to knights who taught them how to ride, fight, and follow the knight's code of conduct, known as chivalry. The daughters of nobles were taught at home how to run the manor, and how to defend it in times of war. The children of serfs, on the other hand, did not get any formal education. They joined their parents in the fields at an early age.

Knights fought on horseback in heavy armor, so preparing for battle was a big job. A knight's servants had to help him into separate pieces of armor for his feet, legs, arms, chest, and head. He even wore metal gloves on his hands. All this armor and a knight's sword could weigh as much as 80 pounds. Knights were very strong, but they still needed help to get up on their horses because of their armor.

The Rise of Towns

Europe's towns began to grow around 1000. Manors had surplus crops to sell in the towns, and lords made the roads safer for traders. Craftworkers in the towns formed **guilds**, organized groups who set prices and rules for their businesses. Serfs moved to the towns as well, because under feudal rules, if they could avoid capture in a town for a year and a day, they were free.

The towns were not pleasant places to live. People threw waste and garbage into the crowded streets. Pigs and rats fed on the garbage and spread disease. The water was polluted, and the streets were full of criminals.

QUICK CHECK

Draw Conclusions **Why did many serfs move to towns even though life was miserable there?**

INVADERS FROM THE NORTH

During the early Middle Ages, one might have heard people praying, "From the fury of the Norsemen, good Lord deliver us." The Norsemen, or "North men," came in ships from northern Europe—today's Denmark, Norway, and Sweden. In surprise attacks, they looted towns and then sailed off. Some Norsemen started a settlement on the northwest coast of France. Today, this area is called Normandy after the "Normans," or Norsemen, who lived there. As happened in other cultures around the world, the Norse invaders began following some of the customs of the places they conquered. Soon, the Normans were French-speaking Christians.

William the Conqueror

The greatest Norman leader was William the Conqueror. King Edward of England promised William that he could become King of England after Edward's death. When Edward died in 1066, William led a Norman army across the English Channel to claim the throne. As king, William took land from English lords and gave it to his Norman knights.

◄ Norsemen warriors sailed south to launch surprise attacks on European towns. They wore helmets made of iron and bronze like this one from Sweden.

William wanted to learn more about the large country he now controlled. So he ordered a census, or official counting, of every person, animal, and manor in the land. Today, William's census gives us an accurate picture of life in England during the early Middle Ages.

The "Great Charter"

One of William's descendants, King John, raised taxes and sent his enemies to prison without fair trials. By 1215, angry English nobles and their soldiers gave John a choice: sign their Magna Carta, or "Great Charter," or lose the throne. The Magna Carta was the first document that gave nobles and other people in England certain basic rights even the king could not take away. For example,

the king could not throw nobles in jail without a fair trial or raise taxes without the nobles' permission.

EVENT

King John never wanted to **sign the Magna Carta** and did not follow most of its rules. He plotted revenge on the nobles who made him sign it. He died before he could act on his plans.

Signing the Magna Carta

QUICK CHECK

Draw Conclusions Why did William the Conqueror want to take a census of his lands?

Check Understanding

1. **VOCABULARY** Use these vocabulary words in a paragraph about the life of serfs in the early Middle Ages.

   feudalism   **manor**   **vassal**

2. **READING SKILL Draw Conclusions** Use the chart from page 180 to draw conclusions about the daily lives of people at each level of feudal society.

Text Clues	Conclusion

3. **Write About It** How did the Norse invasions change European civilization?

   Essential Question

The *Middle Ages* and the Church

VOCABULARY

monastery p. 187

convent p. 187

cathedral p. 187

Crusade p. 188

READING SKILL

Draw Conclusions

Why was the Black Death able to spread so quickly and easily in Europe?

Text Clues	Conclusion

STANDARDS FOCUS

SOCIAL STUDIES Global Connections

GEOGRAPHY Environment and Society

The Amiens Cathedral in France

Essential Question

Why are the Middle Ages called the Age of Faith?

A By 1000, most Europeans were Christians, and the church had great power.

B Popes urged Christians to join in Crusades to capture Jerusalem.

C A plague called the Black Death helped to end the Age of Faith.

THE AGE OF FAITH

By the year 1000, most people in Europe had become Christians. As the church grew stronger, it took a role in most parts of people's daily lives. This is why the Middle Ages is sometimes called the Age of Faith.

For years, the popes of Rome clashed with the Christian leaders of the Byzantine Empire over who should lead the worldwide Catholic church. Finally, in 1054, the church split. There was one leader in Constantinople, for what would become known as the Eastern Orthodox Church. The pope in Rome continued to lead western European churches.

The Role of Monks

During the Middle Ages, some men became monks, men who live in a religious community called a **monastery**. Nuns, or women who chose to live a life devoted to religion, lived in communities called **convents**. Monks and nuns were dedicated to prayer and learning. Most monasteries and convents grew or made everything the people living in them needed.

Monasteries housed the few schools that existed in Europe. Monks and nuns who learned to read and write were among the most educated people in Europe. Many monks carefully copied and illustrated ancient religious texts, as well as ancient Greek and Roman works. They helped preserve important ideas for future European scientists and thinkers.

The Rise of Cathedrals

As European towns grew wealthy, they showed their faith by building great churches, or **cathedrals**. A cathedral is led by a bishop, a religious leader who controls many smaller churches. It took many years—and a lot of money—to build a cathedral. One cathedral in Cologne, Germany, took more than 600 years to finish! Skilled workers illustrated events from the Bible on beautiful stained-glass windows.

QUICK CHECK

Draw Conclusions **How did monks contribute to society in the Middle Ages?**

▼ By copying old books, monks preserved ancient knowledge.

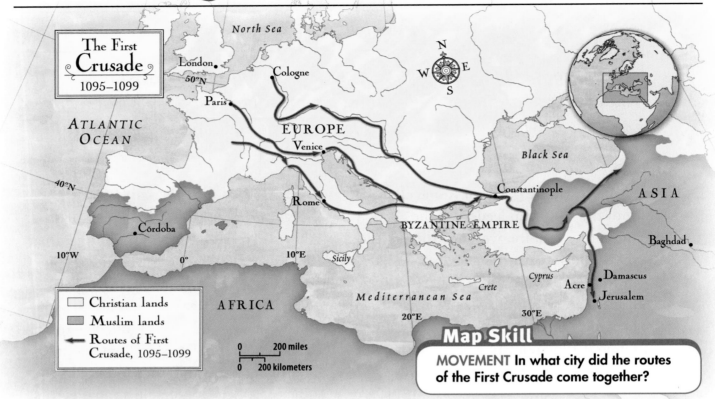

The First Crusade 1095–1099

North Sea

London
Cologne
50°N
Paris
EUROPE
ATLANTIC OCEAN
40°N
Venice
Rome
Córdoba
10°W
0°
10°E
Sicily
BYZANTINE EMPIRE
Black Sea
Constantinople
ASIA
Baghdad
Cyprus
Crete
Acre
Damascus
Jerusalem
Mediterranean Sea
AFRICA
20°E
30°E

☐ Christian lands
▨ Muslim lands
← Routes of First Crusade, 1095–1099

0   200 miles
0   200 kilometers

Map Skill

MOVEMENT **In what city did the routes of the First Crusade come together?**

In 1071, the Seljuk Turks, Muslim soldiers from Central Asia, captured Jerusalem. The city was holy to Jews, Christians, and Muslims. Christians had been making pilgrimages, or religious journeys, to Jerusalem for years. Europeans worried that the Muslim Turks would stop Christian pilgrimages to the city.

The Christian leaders of the Byzantine Empire had split from the church in Rome years before. But now they asked the pope for help in fighting the Turks. In 1095, Pope Urban II called on European Christians to march to Jerusalem to take the city.

As many as 100,000 Christians answered the pope's call. Although some were knights, most were working men and women, children, and elderly people. These Christians believed God had called them to fight a holy war, later called a **Crusade**. The soldiers were called Crusaders.

Many Crusaders wore a red cross on their clothes as a sign of their obedience to the pope's call. Their journey was difficult and badly planned. They traveled by foot or on boats. Almost half of them died of hunger or sickness before they reached Jerusalem. Many others got lost along the way.

The Crusaders who survived the journey reached Jerusalem in 1099. In a bloody one-month battle, they captured the city. After their victory, most of the Crusaders went home to Europe and their families.

Christians lost control of Jerusalem less than 100 years after the First Crusade. Muslim forces led by a general named Saladin recaptured the city in 1187. Popes called for nine Crusades in all, but by 1291, all the lands won by the first Crusaders were back under Muslim control.

Crusades Change Europe

The Crusades caused many changes in European society. With the encouragement of the church, many nobles sold their estates, freed their serfs, and marched off to war. Also, port cities on the Mediterranean Sea, like Venice, grew as they became important stops for traveling Crusaders.

The Crusaders saw places they had never dreamed of. When they returned home, they told amazing stories of the new inventions and great cities of the Muslim world.

Marco Polo

In 1271, near the end of the Crusades, a young explorer from Venice named Marco Polo traveled the entire length of the Silk Road—the trade route that linked China to the

Mediterranean Sea. Then he stayed in China for 21 years. When Polo returned home, he shared amazing tales of his adventures. Polo inspired other Europeans to travel the Silk Road themselves, which increased trade with China.

QUICK CHECK

Draw Conclusions **Why would serfs decide to join the Crusades?**

Marco Polo began his journey to Asia from Venice in 1271. ▶

Marco Polo

189

DataGraphic

The Plague

The chart below shows how the population of Europe changed during the plague years. The map shows when the Black Death reached different regions of Europe.

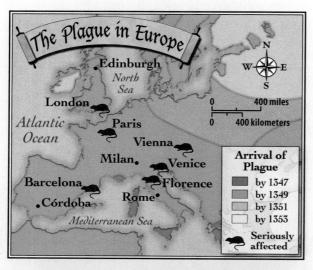

The Plague in Europe

Edinburgh
North Sea
London
Atlantic Ocean
Paris
Vienna
Milan
Venice
Barcelona
Florence
Córdoba
Rome
Mediterranean Sea

N W E S

0 400 miles
0 400 kilometers

Arrival of Plague
by 1347
by 1349
by 1351
by 1353
Seriously affected

Population of Europe 1300-1500

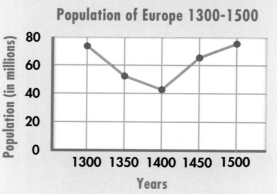

Population (in millions)

80
60
40
20
0

1300 1350 1400 1450 1500

Years

Think About the Plague

1. How long did it take for the plague to spread across Europe?

2. How was life in Europe in 1400 different from life there in 1300?

In the 1300s, a plague struck Europe. A plague is a terrible disease that spreads quickly. It was called the Black Death, and it killed millions of people. Today, scientists believe the disease was the bubonic plague, which is carried from rats to humans by fleas. European cities of the time were filled with rats and fleas, and many people were exposed to the illness.

The plague probably began in the Gobi Desert in Asia and spread west along the Silk Road. It struck Asia in the 1330s, killing millions of people in China and the Middle East. By 1347, the Black Death had reached Europe. At least one in three Europeans, about 38 million people in all, died from the plague. The plague affected Europeans for 130 years.

One writer, Robert Avesbury, described life in England during the plague years:

"Those marked for death were scarce permitted to live longer than three or four days. It showed favor to no one, except a very few of the wealthy. On the same day, 20, 40, or 60 bodies, and on many occasions many more, might be committed for burial together in the same pit."

Serfs No More

The death of so many millions of people changed Europe's economy. As demand for food dropped, prices for farm goods fell. Trade also declined because many merchants died while they traveled. So many serfs died that lords had to begin to pay workers to plant their crops. Serfs then began to ask for higher pay and freedom from their lords. Some of these workers used their wages to rent their own land and earn more money. These changes sped up the end of feudalism in Europe.

QUICK CHECK

Draw Conclusions **How did the Black Death change life for lords?**

Check Understanding

1. **VOCABULARY** Use these words in a paragraph about the role of religion during the Middle Ages.

   monastery   cathedral

   convent   Crusade

2. **READING SKILL** Draw Conclusions Use the chart from page 186 to explain why the Black Death was able to spread so quickly and easily in Europe.

Text Clues	Conclusion

Essential Question 3. **Write About It** How did the Crusades change Europe?

◀ **A doctor tries to help a plague patient by treating the sores that were a symptom of the disease.**

RENAISSANCE AND REFORMATION

Lesson 3

VOCABULARY

Renaissance p. 193

humanism p. 193

Inquisition p. 197

Reformation p. 198

annul p. 199

READING SKILL

Draw Conclusions

How can art and writing change a civilization?

Text Clues	Conclusion

STANDARDS FOCUS

SOCIAL STUDIES Individuals, Groups, and Institutions

GEOGRAPHY Human Systems

In this painting, "The Procession of the Magi," by Benozzo Gozzoli, the young man on the horse is Lorenzo the Magnificent.

Essential Question

How did new ideas and conflicts change Europe?

 **A** Artists and thinkers were supported by rulers like the Medicis of Italy.

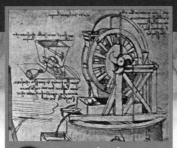 **B** Leonardo da Vinci changed people's ideas about art and science.

 **C** France and England fought the Hundred Years' War.

 **D** Europe's Christians split into two religious groups.

A TIME FOR NEW IDEAS

The plague caused terrible suffering in Europe. For 130 years, people had lived with death and despair every day. Now that the plague had ended, the people were ready for something new.

A period called the **Renaissance** began in Italy around 1350. *Renaissance* is a French word meaning "rebirth." During the Renaissance, many people began to study and value art, literature, and science. This sparked a rebirth of many ideas that had been lost since Greek and Roman times.

The Renaissance began in the northern Italian city-state of Florence. By 1400, Florence had become one of the strongest and wealthiest of Italy's independent city-states. Florentine craftworkers produced wool fabrics and other goods that attracted customers from all over the world. Florence was a major trading center for goods from Asia, Africa, and Europe.

The most important family in Florence was the Medicis, who were powerful bankers. By 1434, the family controlled Florence's government. Some Medicis even became popes.

The powerful Florentine ruler Lorenzo de Medici, or Lorenzo the Magnificent, invited artists and scholars to the city. He paid them well, and they created many new artworks, often featuring members of the Medici family.

Renaissance Ideas and Writings

Scholars in Florence and elsewhere began to study humans and the world they lived in. This way of thinking was called **humanism**. Humanist ideas were inspired by ancient Greek and Roman writings. Muslim and Jewish scholars had copied, translated, and added to Greek and Roman ideas for hundreds of years. Now European thinkers began to build on these ideas as well.

Humanist writers tried to re-create classical styles. Francesco Petrarch, the most famous Renaissance poet, lived in Italy. He is most famous for a group of 366 poems to his love, Laura.

QUICK CHECK

Draw Conclusions Why did the Medicis support the arts?

The Ponte Vecchio bridge in Florence ▼

RENAISSANCE ART AND SCIENCE

The great humanist artists and thinkers were interested in so many different ideas at once that the term "Renaissance man" was used to describe them. The term means someone who is curious about everything. Artist, scientist, and engineer Leonardo da Vinci is the best known Renaissance man. His most famous painting is of the *Mona Lisa*, a woman with a mysterious half-smile. It is now in a museum in Paris.

Painter and sculptor Michelangelo Buonarroti was another important Renaissance man. Michelangelo is famous for the painting he created on the ceiling of the Sistine Chapel in the Vatican in Rome. The Vatican is the headquarters of the Catholic church and home of the pope. Michelangelo painted the ceiling while lying on his back on a high platform. It took him four years to finish the ceiling.

◄ Leonardo da Vinci's "The Lady with the Ermine"

ART

Lorenzo de Medici recognized young **Leonardo da Vinci's** talent and moved the artist into his palace in Florence. Da Vinci loved Florence. In its streets and its people, he found many subjects for his paintings.

German **Albrecht Durer** traveled to Italy twice and learned a great deal from Italian Renaissance artists. In his paintings, prints, and woodcuts, like his famous rhinoceros, Durer combined new Italian ideas with northern European traditions of highly detailed artwork.

Albrecht Durer's famous drawing of a rhinoceros (c. 1515) ▲

People were amazed by **Michelangelo's** paintings and sculptures because they were so realistic. His subjects had bulging muscles and lifelike facial expressions, and his style influenced many other Renaissance artists. His most famous sculpture, of the Biblical king David, can still be seen in Florence today.

◄ Michelangelo's statue of David

A Revolution in Science

For hundreds of years, religious leaders had taught Europeans that Earth was the center of the universe. Then astronomer Nicolaus Copernicus realized that Earth could not be the center of the universe. He discovered that the Earth, as well as the other planets in the solar system, had to revolve around the sun. Many Europeans refused to believe Copernicus. No one would print his ideas until the year he died, 1543, when his book, *On the Revolutions of the Heavenly Spheres*, was finally published. His ideas—which were proven and expanded on by later scientists like Johannes Kepler, Galileo Galilei, and Isaac Newton—would change humanity's knowledge about Earth and the universe.

QUICK CHECK

Draw Conclusions **Why might religious and political leaders have rejected Copernicus's ideas?**

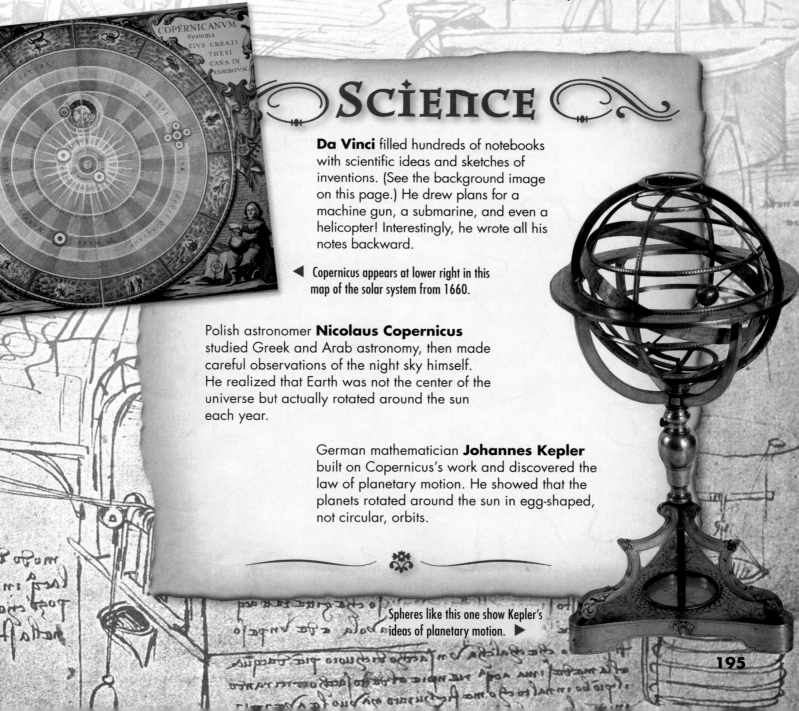

SCIENCE

Da Vinci filled hundreds of notebooks with scientific ideas and sketches of inventions. (See the background image on this page.) He drew plans for a machine gun, a submarine, and even a helicopter! Interestingly, he wrote all his notes backward.

◄ Copernicus appears at lower right in this map of the solar system from 1660.

Polish astronomer **Nicolaus Copernicus** studied Greek and Arab astronomy, then made careful observations of the night sky himself. He realized that Earth was not the center of the universe but actually rotated around the sun each year.

German mathematician **Johannes Kepler** built on Copernicus's work and discovered the law of planetary motion. He showed that the planets rotated around the sun in egg-shaped, not circular, orbits.

Spheres like this one show Kepler's ideas of planetary motion. ►

WAR IN FRANCE AND SPAIN

▲ The Hundred Years' War lasted from 1337 to 1453.

While the Renaissance thrived in Italy, France and England fought a series of battles that lasted so long they are called the Hundred Years' War.

Ongoing quarrels over French land held by England's kings turned into war in 1337. King Edward III of England, whose mother was a French princess, marched into France and declared himself its king. The French did not want an English ruler, and the fighting began. For more than a century, territory in France went from English to French control and back again. In 1453, France finally defeated the English. England lost all its French lands except for the city of Calais.

The war was expensive for both countries and left much of France in ruins. The fighting helped to unite people within both France and England. As they pushed for victory against a common enemy, the English and French kingdoms became nations, or communities of people who share not only the same territory, but the same political, economic, and cultural goals as well.

Joan of Arc

During the war, in 1429, a teenage peasant named Joan of Arc told Prince Charles, ruler of southern France, that saints had told her to lead his troops into battle to capture the city of Orléans from the English. Charles agreed with the plan. Joan rode on horseback in front of the French troops, offering encouragement to the soldiers. The French succeeded and took Orléans in nine days. Soon after, however, the English captured Joan, charged her with witchcraft, and sentenced the 19-year-old to death. In 1920, she was made a saint by the Roman Catholic Church.

The End of Muslim Spain

You have read about how Muslims from North Africa conquered most of Spain and Portugal in the 700s. The Muslims were tolerant of some religions. They allowed Jews and Christians to worship in their own way.

Spanish church leaders wanted the entire region to be Christian, however, and their troops began to push the Muslims out. By 1300, Muslims held only a small part of southern Spain, around the city-state of Granada. In 1469, Princess Isabella of Castile married Prince Ferdinand of Aragon. The two leaders then combined their forces and conquered Granada in 1492. Their victory was the end of Muslim rule in Spain.

Terror in Spain

As king and queen of Spain, Ferdinand and Isabella wanted to close their country to anyone who was not Christian. First they drove out the Muslims, and then Jews were forced to leave as well. Some Jews stayed, however, and tried to practice their religion secretly. To find these people, Ferdinand and Isabella used the **Inquisition**, a church-run court. The officers of the Inquisition investigated people suspected of not being Christian and either drove them out of the country or killed them. The Inquisition helped Ferdinand and Isabella create a Christian country. Spain's culture and economy suffered, however, from the loss of so many citizens.

QUICK CHECK

Summarize **How did Ferdinand and Isabella change Spain?**

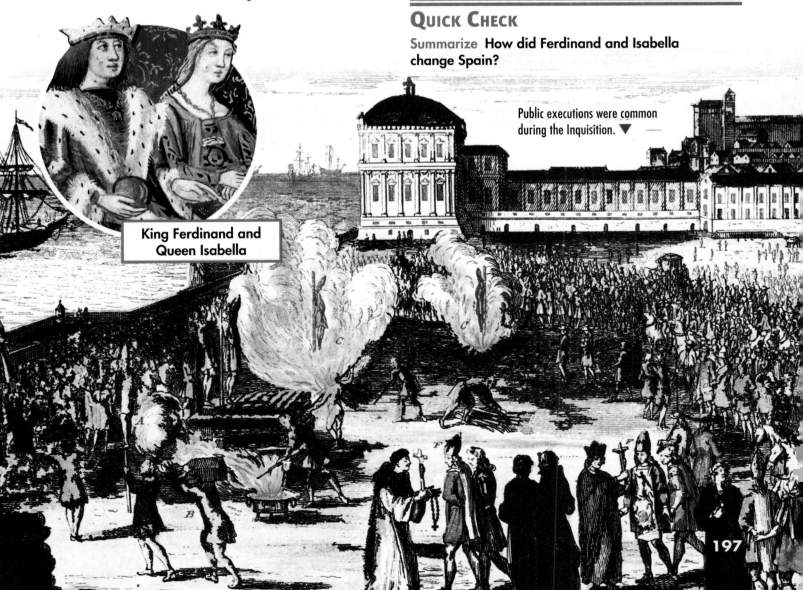

King Ferdinand and Queen Isabella

Public executions were common during the Inquisition. ▼

D CHALLENGING THE CHURCH

During the Renaissance, the Catholic Church took a role in areas of daily life beyond religion. Some popes and bishops became powerful political rulers. Martin Luther, a German monk, was upset about the church's interest in worldly things. He was especially angry that the church sold indulgences. An indulgence is a forgiveness of sins.

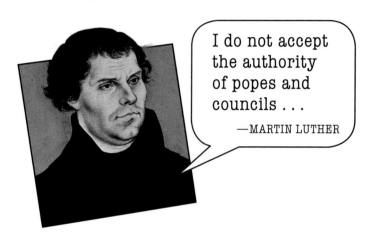

I do not accept the authority of popes and councils . . .
—MARTIN LUTHER

Luther wrote Ninety-five Theses, or arguments, about why the church needed to change its practices. In 1517, he nailed them to the door of his local church. By doing so, he started the **Reformation**, a movement to reform, or change, the church.

Luther's ideas spread quickly with the help of the printing press. Chinese and Arab printers had been using printing presses and movable type for many years. Movable type used interchangeable letters to form words. A German named Johannes Gutenberg built the first European printing press that used metal moveable type. Now pages could be printed more quickly and cheaply than earlier methods. Luther's ideas were printed on Gutenberg presses. In 1520, the pope ordered Luther's books burned. Church leaders wanted to punish Luther, but German leaders protected him.

Luther's followers were called Protestants because they left the Catholic church to protest its practices. Protestants prayed in their own languages, instead of Latin. They did not have monasteries and convents, and their churches did not accept the leadership of the pope.

Following the Reformation, the church in Rome became known as the Roman Catholic Church. Roman Catholics began a reform movement called the Counter-Reformation in 1545. Catholic leaders agreed to begin offering parts of their church services in languages other than Latin and to change other church practices.

One of the Bibles printed by Gutenberg ▼

A new Globe Theatre was built in London in 1997.

Changes in England

England's King Henry VIII had no sons who could become king after him. In 1533, Henry asked the pope to **annul**, or legally undo, his marriage so he could remarry and try to have a son with a new queen. When the pope refused, Henry left the Catholic Church. He declared himself head of the Church of England, or the Anglican Church, and divorced his wife.

King Henry did remarry, but he had a daughter, Elizabeth, not a son. During her reign, William Shakespeare began producing his plays at the Globe Theatre. Shakespeare based his plays on ancient Greek and Roman stories, as well as on English history. His actors often performed for Queen Elizabeth.

QUICK CHECK

Draw Conclusions **Why was it difficult for the pope to stop the Reformation?**

Check Understanding

1. **VOCABULARY** Use these words in a paragraph about changes in the church.

   annul   **Inquisition**   **Reformation**

2. **READING SKILL** Draw Conclusions Use your chart from page 192 to explain how art and writing can change a civilization.

Text Clues	Conclusion

   Essential Question 3. **Write About It** How did Gutenberg's printing press change life in Europe?

China's Dynasties

Lesson 4

VOCABULARY

porcelain p. 202

abacus p. 202

Forbidden City p. 203

READING SKILL

Draw Conclusions

How did voyages of exploration benefit China during the Ming dynasty?

Text Clues	Conclusion

STANDARDS FOCUS

SOCIAL STUDIES — Time, Continuity, and Change

GEOGRAPHY — The Uses of Geography

The Great Wall of China is nearly 4,000 miles long.

Essential Question

What were some events of later Chinese dynasties?

A Under the Tang dynasty, China grew powerful and wealthy.

B China became a large empire and encouraged voyages of exploration.

C China turned inward in the 1600s and closed its doors to the West.

A A NEW CHINESE DYNASTY

It is New Year's Day. The emperor rides in a procession of 5,000 elephants, covered with embroidered silk. An official calls out, "Bow down and worship." Generals, nobles, and even ambassadors from other lands bow until their foreheads touch the ground.

The fall of the Han dynasty in China in A.D. 200 was followed by almost 400 years of conflict. Then, in 618, the Tang dynasty reunited China and expanded it west of the Huang He and south to Vietnam. The Great Wall kept out enemies from the north, and the Grand Canal, the largest in the ancient world, helped build trade within China. Tang rulers also welcomed foreign traders to China.

A new school of Buddhism, Chan, developed during the Tang dynasty. Chan emphasized the relationship between a pupil and teacher. You may have heard Chan called by its Japanese name—Zen Buddhism.

A Female Emperor

The first woman to lead China, Wu Hou, ruled during the Tang dynasty. She filled her government with scholars who had passed civil service exams—not just nobles. She also lowered the taxes paid by peasant farmers.

After Empress Wu was forced from the throne, the Chinese Empire declined and its borders shrank. Tang rule ended in about 900, and China faced chaos again.

QUICK CHECK

Draw Conclusions **Why did Wu Hou prefer scholars as officials, instead of nobles?**

Tang and Yuan China

ARCTIC OCEAN

EUROPE
Moscow
Constantinople

ASIA

Tigris River
Samarkand
Beijing
JAPAN
Huang He
PACIFIC OCEAN

Guangzhou

Arabian Sea
INDIA

0   500   1,000 miles
0   500 1,000 kilometers

— Tang Dynasty, 618–c.900
▢ Yuan Dynasty, c. 1200–1400

Map Skill

LOCATION **About how many miles from Beijing is Moscow?**

The entrance gate to the Forbidden City opens onto Tiananmen Square in Beijing.

ⓑ LATER DYNASTIES

Around 960, the Song dynasty restored order to China. During the Song period, artists painted beautiful landscapes and produced delicate **porcelain**, a type of fine pottery. Song Chinese also invented movable type, making it possible to print books. At this time, many Chinese could read and write. In fact, until about 1800, there were more printed books in China than in any other place in the world.

Chinese merchants made calculations using the **abacus**, a counting device with several columns of beads. By moving the beads, merchants could add and subtract quickly. Merchants also began to accept paper money. Under the Song, the Chinese also invented a compass and gunpowder and built the largest ships in the world. Later Song rulers were weak, however, and invaders from Mongolia ended the Song dynasty in 1279.

Yuan Dynasty

In 1206, Mongol leader Genghis Khan began a series of conquests. He had captured most of northern China by the time of his death in 1227. His grandson, Kublai Khan, conquered southern China and began the Yuan dynasty. The Yuan eventually controlled the largest empire, by territory, in the history of the world. It stretched from today's Ukraine to the Pacific Ocean. Kublai Khan's soldiers patrolled the Silk Road. Yuan paper money was accepted by merchants throughout Asia because they knew it would not lose its value.

Europeans knew about Kublai Khan from a book written by Marco Polo. The Venetian trader and adventurer arrived in China in 1271 and lived there for 21 years. Europeans loved his stories of Chinese cities, the Yuan court, and Mongol armies.

The Ming Dynasty

Over time, the Yuan rulers grew weaker and, in 1368, the Ming Dynasty replaced them. Ming rulers rebuilt the Great Wall in the form that visitors to China can see today. Under Emperor Yong Le, the Ming began building the Imperial City within the capital city of Beijing. Gardens, lakes, and over 1,000 buildings, including palaces, libraries, and temples, were inside the city's red walls. It became known as the **Forbidden City,** because common people could not enter it.

At that time, the Ming navy was the world's largest and most powerful. Yong Le sent an admiral named Zheng He on seven voyages of exploration, beginning in 1405. Zheng He led a fleet of over 60 ships, some of which were more than 400 feet long. The fleet carried Chinese products and created foreign markets for silk, porcelain, and other goods. Zheng He returned to China with spices from India and exotic animals from Africa, including two giraffes.

The next emperor, however, abandoned the powerful Chinese navy and its explorations. The great ships rotted at their docks, and China turned away from the outside world.

QUICK CHECK

Cause and Effect What was one important effect of the voyages of Zheng He?

Both the bowl and wall tiles feature dragons, the symbol of the Ming Dynasty.

● CHINA AND THE WEST

For many years, Chinese technology and culture were the most advanced in the world. China did not maintain its lead, however. By 1800, Europe had more advanced technology, a change you will read about later.

In 1644, the Ming dynasty was overthrown by the Manchus, a people from eastern China. The Manchus began the Qing dynasty. Their soldiers added Tibet, Mongolia, and the island of Taiwan to their empire. Qing rulers believed that all non-Chinese people were inferior, and they limited China's contact with the rest of the world. They had no interest in learning about technology from other countries.

Decline of the Qing

By the middle of the 1800s, the Qing had lost control of China. A revolt by peasants spread across southern China and destroyed much of the land. Soon after, China lost a war with Britain and was forced to open some of its ports to foreign trade. By 1900, France, Japan, Germany, Russia, and the United States had each sent ships to claim the rights to trade in large sections of the country. The world had come to China.

QUICK CHECK

Draw Conclusions **How might government decisions have caused China's decline in the mid-1800s?**

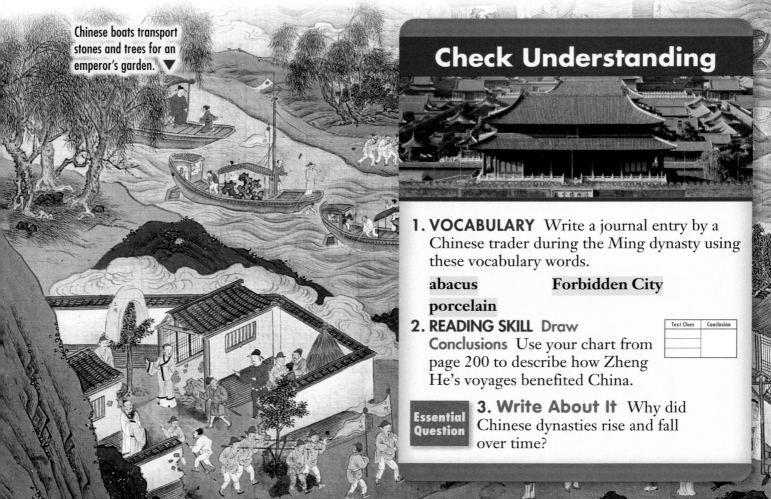

Chinese boats transport stones and trees for an emperor's garden. ▼

Check Understanding

1. **VOCABULARY** Write a journal entry by a Chinese trader during the Ming dynasty using these vocabulary words.

   abacus   **Forbidden City**

   porcelain

2. **READING SKILL** Draw Conclusions Use your chart from page 200 to describe how Zheng He's voyages benefited China.

Text Clues	Conclusion

3. **Write About It** Why did Chinese dynasties rise and fall over time?

   Essential Question

Chart and Graph Skills

Use Flow Charts

VOCABULARY

flow chart

A **flow chart** uses pictures or words to show, step-by-step, how something is made or done. The flow chart below shows the steps involved in making silk fabric. Look at it as you follow the steps.

Learn It

- A flow chart uses boxes of words, pictures, or both to describe each step in a process.

- The title shows the topic of the flow chart.

- Arrows or numbers show the order of the steps.

Try It

- What is the first step in making silk?

- Use the flow chart to write a paragraph describing how silk is made in a Chinese factory.

Apply It

- Make a flow chart showing each step involved in something that you make or do every day.

MAKING SILK

1  Silkworm cocoons are sorted in a Chinese factory.

2  Women boil silkworm cocoons to unravel their silk.

3  A worker spins cocoon silk into silk thread.

4  Cloth is woven from the silk threads.

The Indian Empire

Lesson 5

VOCABULARY
Mogul p. 207

shah p. 208

READING SKILL
Draw Conclusions

How did changes in Mogul culture make the Taj Mahal possible?

Text Clues	Conclusion

STANDARDS FOCUS

SOCIAL STUDIES Power, Authority, and Governance

GEOGRAPHY Places and Regions

Akbar the Great meets with his advisers.

Essential Question

How did Mogul rule change India?

A The Mogul Empire began in 1526 and controlled most of what is today India.

B The arts thrived during the Mogul Empire.

A NEW RULERS IN INDIA

Akbar was named "great," but the prince did not have a great start in life. He was born while his royal parents were hiding from their enemies. He grew up to rule an empire for 49 years.

Centuries after the early Indian empires fell, Muslim invaders from the north and west conquered most of the Indus River Valley. The region's new sultans built their capital in Delhi, near today's Indian capital, New Delhi. In 1526, a new conqueror, Babur, captured the Indus River Valley. He claimed his ancestors included Genghis Khan. Babur's empire was known as the **Mogul** Empire. The word *Mogul* refers to Persian, Mongolian, or Turkish Muslims who lived in India.

In 1556, Babur's grandson, Akbar, became emperor when he was only 13. By that time, the Mogul Empire had become weak and war-torn. Akbar had to fight to keep his power, and by age 19, he was leading armies into battle. He became a brilliant general and soon took complete control of the empire.

A Tolerant Emperor

The Muslim rulers before Akbar had not allowed Hindus to build new temples, and Hindus also had to pay higher taxes than Muslims. Akbar, who married a Hindu princess, reversed these policies and let Hindus practice their religion freely. He also brought Hindus, such as his father-in-law, into important government positions. This tolerance was unusual for the time and made Akbar respected by Indians of all religions.

QUICK CHECK

Draw Conclusions Why was Akbar popular with people throughout his empire?

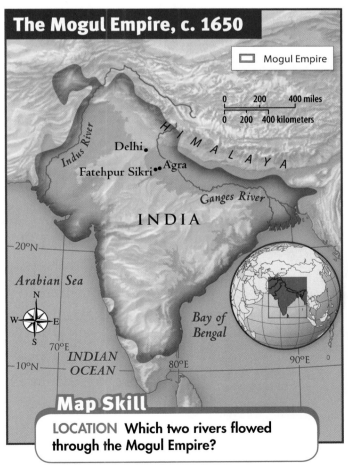

The Mogul Empire, c. 1650

Mogul Empire

0   200   400 miles
0   200   400 kilometers

Indus River
Delhi
HIMALAYA
Fatehpur Sikri • Agra
Ganges River
INDIA
20°N
Arabian Sea
N
W   E
S
70°E
INDIAN OCEAN
10°N
80°E
Bay of Bengal
90°E

Map Skill

LOCATION Which two rivers flowed through the Mogul Empire?

B LIFE DURING THE MOGUL EMPIRE

During his long reign, Akbar ruled much of India and Afghanistan. He changed the tax system so that wealthy farmers paid higher taxes than poor farmers. He created a central money system to encourage trade, and he supervised building projects, such as wells and irrigation canals. Akbar was so busy that he seldom slept more than three hours a night.

Akbar built a spectacular new capital city called Fatehpur Sikri, which means "city of victory." The water source for this magnificent city dried up quickly, however, so Akbar had to move his capital to Agra. You can still visit Fatehpur Sikri today. It is a perfectly preserved city, but it's also silent and empty.

Mogul Culture

The arts thrived under Akbar. He set up workshops in his palace to support the best artists and craftworkers in the empire. Akbar loved paintings and paid artists to create a massive work called the "Hamzanama." It was made up of 1,400 large paintings. Other craftworkers produced beautiful textiles, carpets, jewelry, and paintings in the palace workshops. Akbar himself often worked beside the artists.

A jeweled hawk from the Mogul period ▼

Akbar collected a large library of Greek, Hindi, Persian, and Arabic books, but he himself never learned to read. Instead, people read to him every day, and he memorized what he heard. He also had his own orchestra of musicians.

Shah Jahan

In 1628, Akbar's grandson Jahan took the throne and ruled for the next 30 years. Jahan took the title **shah**, which means "king" in Persian. Europeans called him "The Great Mogul." Shah Jahan loved luxury and splendor. His six-foot tall throne was made of marble and solid gold and was covered with diamonds, rubies, emeralds, and other precious stones. The throne got its name, the "Peacock Throne," because there was a pair of peacock figures standing behind it. The throne was twice as valuable as the palace it sat in. After Jahan's time, the term "Peacock Throne" referred to the kings of Persia (today's Iran).

The Taj Mahal

When Shah Jahan's beloved wife, Mumtaz Mahal, died in 1631, the king planned the most spectacular tomb in the world for her. The finest craftworkers in the empire worked on her tomb, the Taj Mahal. It took more than 20 years and 20,000 workers to build the white marble structure. Today, the magnificent 20-story monument they produced is a national symbol of India.

The shah could afford to build such a tomb because trade was booming. Cotton from India clothed people in Asia, Africa, and Europe. Indians sold spices and silk directly to merchants from Portugal, England, and the Netherlands. The shah also raised money by increasing the land taxes peasants had to pay.

▲ Shah Jahan built the Taj Mahal (above), for his beloved wife, Mumtaz Mahal (left).

Fall of the Moguls

After Shah Jahan's death, his son destroyed Hindu temples and restored laws requiring Hindus to pay higher taxes. Hindus rebelled and began a civil war. During the war, in 1739, a powerful Persian army invaded and defeated the Moguls. The empire was reduced to a small area around Delhi.

Europeans had been trading in India since the late 1600s. After the Persians defeated the Moguls, Europeans began building their own trading settlements on Indian land. The Moguls were too weak to stop them. By 1800, the British traders of the East India Company had so much power in India that they even began collecting taxes in some areas.

QUICK CHECK

Draw Conclusions **Why were European countries able to seize Mogul territory?**

Check Understanding

1. **VOCABULARY** Write a description of the Indian empire using these words.

   Mogul   **shah**

2. **READING SKILL** Draw Conclusions Use the chart from page 206 to explain how changes in Mogul culture made the Taj Mahal possible.

Text Clues	Conclusion

3. **Write About It** How did Akbar change Indian civilization?

   Essential Question

209

Feudal Japan

VOCABULARY

Shinto p. 211

shogun p. 211

shogunate p. 212

daimyo p. 212

samurai p. 212

READING SKILL

Draw Conclusions
Use the chart to draw conclusions about how cultural life in Japan changed under the shoguns.

Text Clues	Conclusion

STANDARDS FOCUS

SOCIAL STUDIES Time, Continuity, and Change

GEOGRAPHY Physical Systems

Himeji Castle in Himeji, Japan

Essential Question

How did Japanese culture develop during the feudal period?

A Japan was ruled by an emperor and a shogun, or military commander.

B The Tokugawa shoguns led a long period of peace and stability.

C Japan's cultural life flourished under the Tokugawa shogunate.

A ANCIENT JAPAN

The armored soldiers who defended Japan's feudal lords were strong, well-trained, and loyal: "Nothing is more important than duty," it was written of them. "Second in importance comes life, and then money."

Japan is an archipelago, or chain of islands, off Asia's east coast. It has four mountainous main islands with few natural resources and little farmland. In its early history, Japan was influenced by China and Korea. Japan's oldest religion, **Shinto**, or "the way of the Gods," teaches that divine spirits rule everything in nature—mountains, trees, the weather, and the seasons. Shinto's followers offer special prayers before planting and harvesting crops. Over the years, Shinto blended with Confucianism and Buddhism in Japan to create a unique culture.

Warrior Leaders

Under Shinto, the ruler of Japan was called the emperor. The Japanese believed that the sun goddess, Ameratsu, was the emperor's ancestor, and so the emperor was considered a god, too.

Beginning in the 800s, the emperor's power and control began to decline. By the 1100s, powerful families were fighting for political control. In 1192, one family won the struggle, and the emperor named its leader, Minamoto Yoritomo, the first **shogun**, or military commander, of Japan.

From this time on, while the emperor remained the spiritual leader of Japan, shoguns led the Japanese government.

QUICK CHECK

Draw Conclusions Why did Japan have both an emperor and a shogun?

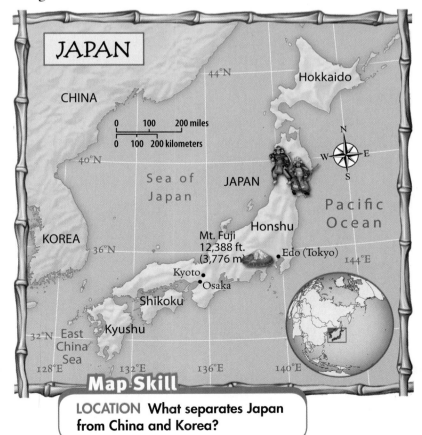

JAPAN

CHINA

44°N

Hokkaido

0   100   200 miles
0   100   200 kilometers

40°N

Sea of Japan

JAPAN

Pacific Ocean

KOREA

36°N

Mt. Fuji
12,388 ft.
(3,776 m)

Honshu

Edo (Tokyo)

144°E

Kyoto

Osaka

Shikoku

32°N East China Sea

Kyushu

128°E   132°E   136°E   140°E

Map Skill

LOCATION What separates Japan from China and Korea?

B THE RULE OF THE SHOGUN

Life in Japan during this period of history, known as the **shogunate**, was based on a feudal system somewhat like Europe's. There were duties and rewards for every member of society. Powerful nobles, or **daimyo**, controlled large pieces of land, which were worked by poor farmers. These nobles and their lands were protected by loyal warriors called **samurai**, who were disciplined and obeyed only their lords. The daimyo themselves swore loyalty to the shogun and provided the shogun with crops and samurai to fight in wars.

The emperor, shogun, daimyo, and samurai were at the top of feudal Japan's social pyramid. Below them were farmers and craft- workers. Merchants were the lowest class, because they were thought to be the least important members of society. It was impossible for anyone to move from one class to another. Farmers or merchants, for example, could not become daimyo or samurai.

All Japanese owed loyalty and obedience to their rulers. When a lord passed through a village, ordinary Japanese were not allowed to look at him. Instead, they fell facedown on the ground to show their respect.

Some Japanese carry rice in baskets while others wash rice in a river. ▼

Japan's rulers had special rights and duties. The daimyos paid no taxes, but they could not marry without the shogun's approval. Also, daimyos were required to give costly gifts to the shogun and to wear expensive clothes. These required expenses were meant to keep any daimyo from becoming too wealthy.

The early shoguns were powerful rulers. Over time, their control weakened. After all, Japan is a long string of islands, and keeping control was not easy. Then, in 1603, the emperor named Tokugawa Ieyasu to be Japan's new shogun. He and his family restored the power of the shogunate by making major changes to Japanese culture.

"The Great Peace"

The Tokugawa shoguns moved Japan's capital from Kyoto to Edo, which is known today as Tokyo. To prevent rebellion, they ruled that only samurai could own weapons. They ordered all daimyo to live in Edo. Nobles could return to their homes only once every

▲ A samurai's suit of armor from the 1100s

two years, and when they did, their families remained in Edo as hostages.

Tokugawa shoguns kept Japan peaceful for more than 250 years. In fact, the Tokugawa Shogunate is known as "the great peace." This peace had a high price, though. Ordinary Japanese had almost no personal freedom.

QUICK CHECK

Draw Conclusions **Why were ordinary Japanese not allowed to look at their rulers?**

C THE CULTURE OF JAPAN

The two most important cities in Japan were Edo and Kyoto. By the 1700s, Edo had a population of more than one million and Kyoto had about 400,000. A 300-mile-long road, the Tokaido, connected the two cities.

Most Japanese families were farmers. Droughts often caused serious crop shortages, which led to famines. As in Europe, many Japanese farm families eventually moved to cities to find work and to escape hunger.

▲ Noh theater masks

In large cities, merchants and craftworkers sold their goods in stalls and shops. Japan had few natural resources, so it was important for people to recycle goods and materials. Some shops repaired old metal pots. Others bought used paper and resold it. Thousands of merchants sold used clothing.

Japan's cities faced constant dangers from fire and natural disasters. Fire was always a worry because so many wooden buildings were crowded together. Earthquakes and volcanoes could also strike at any time.

High Drama and Literature

Edo was the cultural center of Japan, and drama was a popular art form. During the reign of the Tokugawas, plays were performed in two styles—kyogen and noh. Kyogen were short comic plays. Noh plays were longer dramas, usually about historical or mythical characters. Noh plays were more formal, and actors in noh theater always wore masks like the ones shown above. A third type of drama, kabuki, appeared in the 1600s. Kabuki stories focused on samurai heroes and the conflicts they faced between duty and freedom. Kabuki is still popular in Japan today.

Primary Sources

"For Genji life had become an unbroken string of problems. . . . If he went on pretending that all was well, then even worse things might lie ahead. Genji thought of the Suma coast. . . . [It] was deserted, save for the huts of fishermen. According to his attendants, however, Suma [was] the home of one mysterious resident: a puppet. And the puppet had powers to make human beings a joyful lot."

from *The Tale of Genji* by Murasaki Shikibu (c. 1000)

Write About It How do the themes of *The Tale of Genji* resemble those of today's novels?

This painted screen shows Portuguese traders arriving in Japan.

Many Japanese could read, so printed books were popular. Books could be rented and returned after they were read. One of the world's first novels, *The Tale of Genji*, was written around the year 1000 by a Japanese noble, Lady Murasaki Shikibu. Her story of Prince Genji tells us a lot about court life at the time. (See the Primary Sources box at left.)

Japan and the West

In the 1500s, Portuguese traders began arriving in Japan. At first, the visitors were welcomed. But by 1635, Tokugawa Iemitsu had decided that European influences were dangerous. He closed Japan to ships or travelers from the rest of the world. Japan remained isolated for more than 200 years.

QUICK CHECK

Draw Conclusions **Why was recycling so important to the Japanese?**

Check Understanding

1. **VOCABULARY** Write a journal entry about a visit to feudal Japan using the following vocabulary words.

Shinto	**shogunate**	**samurai**
shogun	**daimyo**	

2. **READING SKILL** Draw Conclusions Use the chart from page 210 to describe how cultural life in Japan changed under the Tokugawas.

Text Clues	Conclusion

   Essential Question **3. Write About It** How did Japan change during the shogunate?

Lesson 7

VOCABULARY

strait p. 217

Wat p. 219

complex p. 219

READING SKILL

Draw Conclusions
What was the role of the king in Khmer society?

Text Clues	Conclusion

STANDARDS FOCUS

SOCIAL STUDIES   Time, Continuity, and Change

GEOGRAPHY   Places and Regions

Southeast Asia

A floating market in Thailand

Essential Question

How did kingdoms rise and fall in Southeast Asia?

A Southeast Asia was strongly influenced by Indian and Chinese cultures.

B The Khmer Empire engaged in large building projects.

C After the fall of the Khmer, a new kingdom rose in today's Thailand.

THE LAND OF SOUTHEAST ASIA

When the great temple opened, the people of the city celebrated. There were colorful flowers everywhere, and beautiful flower-filled pools surrounded the building. Every wall was covered with magnificent carvings. The people sang songs about their achievement.

Southeast Asia has two geographical regions. A peninsula runs from China to the Strait of Malacca. A **strait** is a narrow channel connecting two larger bodies of water. There is also an archipelago that includes the island nations of the Philippines and Indonesia. The tropical climate of Southeast Asia is warm and wet, making it especially good for growing rice, the staple of the Southeast Asian diet.

Many Cultures

Southeast Asia developed its own culture, influenced by China and India. Chinese and Indian merchants began traveling to the region about 2,000 years ago. They brought their cultures along with their trade goods. Today, many Southeast Asians are either Hindu or Buddhist—two major religions from India.

Trade played an important role in the development of Southeast Asia. Several Indonesian kingdoms became wealthy by controlling sea routes in the region, especially those used in the valuable spice trade. The largest kingdom in this trade was Java. The island kingdoms were the "spice islands" that Christopher Columbus had hoped to reach when he sailed across the Atlantic Ocean from Spain in 1492.

QUICK CHECK

Draw Conclusions How did control of sea routes benefit Indonesian kingdoms?

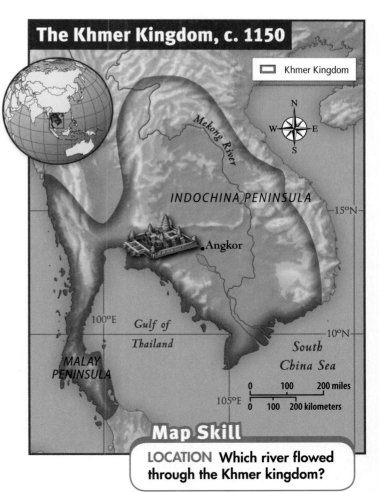

The Khmer Kingdom, c. 1150

Khmer Kingdom

Mekong River

INDOCHINA PENINSULA

15°N

Angkor

100°E   Gulf of Thailand

10°N

South China Sea

MALAY PENINSULA

105°E

0   100   200 miles
0   100   200 kilometers

Map Skill

LOCATION Which river flowed through the Khmer kingdom?

THE KHMER KINGDOM

About 2,000 years ago, the Khmer people had settled along the banks of the Mekong River, which flows southeast through present-day Laos, Cambodia, and Vietnam into the South China Sea. In the 800s, a Khmer ruler named Jayavarman II united his people and began to build a regional empire. For many years, the empire was the most powerful kingdom in Southeast Asia. At the height of its power, the Khmer Empire included Cambodia and parts of today's Vietnam, Laos, and Thailand.

Khmer kings claimed to be the human form of Shiva, a Hindu god. These "god-kings" led their armies into battle. They also ordered the building of roads and reservoirs for floodwaters. Canals were constructed to carry water from reservoirs to the rice fields. The extensive water system helped produce large harvests.

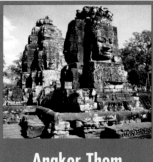

PLACES

The giant Buddhist temple at the center of **Angkor Thom** is famous for its many smiling "face towers." They rise to the central peak of the complex.

Angkor Thom

Enormous Temples

Around 1100, Khmer King Suryavarman II ordered the building of a massive Hindu temple near his capital. The temple, Angkor Wat, required as much stone to build as the Great Pyramid in Egypt. Angkor Wat comes from two Khmer words. Angkor means

Angkor Wat ▶

"holy or capital city" and **Wat** is a temple or monastery. Angkor Wat is actually part of a temple **complex**, or group of buildings, covering about one square mile. Its walls are covered with carvings from Hindu sacred texts. The complex also had an astronomical observatory to study the stars.

Suryavarman's grandson, Jayavarman VII, was a Buddhist. In 1181, he ordered the building of an even larger temple in his capital, Angkor Thom, to honor the Buddha. Even though they are in ruins, you can still visit both temple complexes today.

QUICK CHECK

Draw Conclusions Why did Jayavarman VII want to build a new temple complex?

Citizenship
Public Works

Khmer rulers ordered their subjects to build roads and reservoirs. These are public works projects, or construction projects on things for public use and usually paid for and run by a government. Building public works is an important responsibility of government. In the United States, the government maintains dams, highways, and bridges, as well as buildings like schools and police stations. Citizens are responsible for keeping public works in good condition and voting on which new projects the government should pay for.

Write About It What public works projects are important to people in your community?

The Khmer kingdom remained powerful for about 400 years. Constant war and building the great temple complexes, however, used up much of the government's wealth. In the 1430s, Thai troops from the north captured and destroyed much of Angkor. The city was abandoned and mostly forgotten for centuries. In the 1860s, a French explorer rediscovered the ruins. Today they are one of the region's major tourist attractions.

The defeated Khmer people moved south on the Mekong River and built a new capital city called Phnom Penh. Today this city is still the capital of the nation of Cambodia.

The Thai set up their own kingdom and capital, Ayutthaya, along the Chao Phraya River. This kingdom became the modern nation of Thailand. The people of western Burma formed the kingdom of Pagan in what is today's Myanmar. Both the Thai and the Burmese were heavily influenced by Indian culture. They set up forms of government, religion, and culture modeled on those of the Indian empires. Meanwhile, along the east coast of Southeast Asia, Chinese culture influenced the people of today's Vietnam.

QUICK CHECK

Draw Conclusions **Why did the Khmer kingdom eventually decline?**

◄ **The Wat Pho Buddhist temple in Bangkok, Thailand**

Check Understanding

1. **VOCABULARY** Write a sentence for each of the vocabulary words.

   strait   Wat   complex

2. **READING SKILL** Draw Conclusions Use your chart from page 216 to explain the role of the king in Khmer society.

Text Clues	Conclusion

   Essential Question 3. **Write About It** How did the Khmer kingdom rise and fall?

Map and Globe Skills

Use Map Projections

VOCABULARY

projection

All flat maps have one big problem: since Earth is curved, the maps can never be completely accurate. Mapmakers have invented ways of drawing the Earth on flat surfaces. These drawings are called **projections**. Each type has advantages and disadvantages. Follow the steps below to learn more about two popular kinds of map projections.

Learn It

- The first map is a Mercator projection. The lines of latitude and longitude are straight, but land areas on either side of the equator are stretched. They look bigger than they really are.

- The second map is a Winkel Tripel projection. The lines of latitude and longitude are curved, so the size of land areas is not distorted. Since the lines are not straight, however, this projection is not good for showing directions.

Try It

Use the maps to answer the questions.

- Which projection most accurately shows the size of landmasses?

- Which projection would you use for finding direction?

Apply It

- Which projection would be better for a map of your town? Why?

Mercator Projection: Southeast Asia

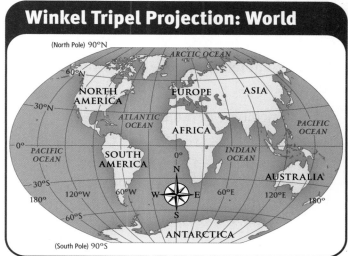

Winkel Tripel Projection: World

Unit 4 Review and Assess

Vocabulary

Write the word from the list that matches each definition below.

abacus   **Renaissance**

annul   **serf**

guild   **strait**

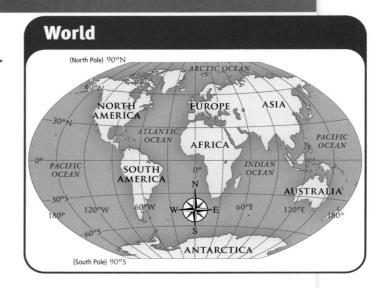

1. organized group of artisans
2. device with sliding beads used for arithmetic
3. farmer bound to work on a noble's land
4. legally undo something
5. narrow waterway that connects larger bodies of water

Comprehension and Critical Thinking

6. How did the fall of Rome change western Europe?

7. Why is the Magna Carta important?

8. **Reading Skill** What conclusion can you draw from European countries claiming the right to trade in China in the 1800s?

9. How were feudal Japan and feudal Europe similar and different?

10. **Critical Thinking** What were the advantages and disadvantages when civilizations undertook massive building projects?

Skill

Use Map Projections

Write a complete sentence to answer each question.

11. Which type of projection is used in this map?

12. Does this map accurately show the size of the world's landmasses? Explain.

Test Preparation

Read the passage. Then answer the questions.

In the 17th century, Japanese artists became famous for their woodblock prints. Chinese printers had begun printing books with woodblocks in the 600s. They cut all of the characters for a page on a block of wood. Then the block was covered with ink, and paper was laid on it to make a print. Japanese artists began making color woodblock prints in a style known as "ukiyo-e," or "picture of the floating world," in about 1600. These prints usually showed scenes of daily life. The most famous ukiyo-e artist was Katsushika Hokusai. His prints influenced later European painters like Edouard Manet and Edgar Degas. In fact, their style was sometimes called "Japonism."

1. Where did people first use woodblocks for printing?

A. Japan
B. China
C. Europe
D. Egypt

2. What was the last step for a Chinese printer?

A. laying paper on the inked block
B. cutting the characters onto a block of wood
C. covering the block with ink
D. none of the above

3. How would you describe a typical ukiyo-e print?

A. showed scenes of daily life
B. used only black and white
C. made in China
D. all of the above

4. Why would woodblock printing be an inefficient method of printing books?

5. Why was the term "Japonism" used to describe the styles of Degas and Manet?

What makes civilizations change?

Write About the Big Idea

Persuasive Essay

In Unit 4, you read about how civilizations change. Use your notes from your foldable to help you write a persuasive essay that answers the Big Idea question, What makes civilizations change? Begin with an introductory paragraph, stating your ideas about what makes civilizations change. Then describe how each civilization changed. Your final paragraph should summarize your main ideas.

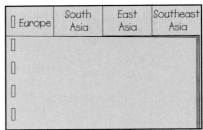

Europe	South Asia	East Asia	Southeast Asia

Create a Poster

Work in small groups to create a poster showing how one or more civilizations changed during the period described in Unit 4. Your poster should use words and pictures to describe the civilization "Before" and "After" major changes. Here's how to make your poster:

1. Research the civilizations of Europe, China, Japan, India, and Southeast Asia and how they changed. Then choose one or more civilizations for your poster.

2. Divide your poster into two sides, "Before" and "After." Have members of your group create pictures showing how your civilization looked before and after major changes.

3. Working as a group, under each picture write paragraphs or lists of ideas describing the civilization "Before" and "After."

4. Share your poster with your class.

Replica of Captains Cook's
ship, Endeavor

The Big Idea

How do new ideas change people's lives?

FOLDABLES™ Study Organizer

Make Inferences
Make an accordion foldable to take notes as you read Unit 5. Your notes will help you answer the Big Idea question. Your foldable's title will be **New Ideas and Changes**. Use one fold for each of the lessons in Unit 5.

LOG ON

For more about Unit 5 go to
www.macmillanmh.com

CHANGING IDEAS

PEOPLE, PLACES, AND EVENTS

Gilbert du Motier, Marquis de Lafayette

Toussaint L'Ouverture

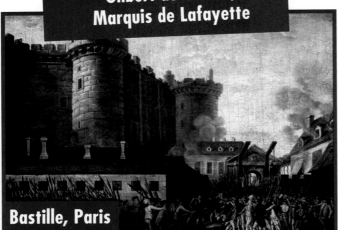

Bastille, Paris

1789
French citizens storm the Bastille in Paris.

Sans Souci, Haiti

1802
Haiti's first ruler built this European-style palace.

1780   1800   1820

The **Marquis de Lafayette** fought for American independence and wanted freedom in his own country, France.

Today you can visit the site of the **Bastille** prison in Paris, where the French Revolution began.

Toussaint L'Ouverture led the armies of Haiti, the second oldest republic in the Americas.

Today you can visit the ruins of a palace built by Henri Christophe, Haiti's first ruler.

LOG ON For more about People, Places, and Events, visit www.macmillanmh.com

Emperor Meiji

Queen Victoria

Imperial Palace, Tokyo

1867
Emperor Meiji moves his government to Tokyo.

Suez Canal, Egypt

1869
European royalty attends the opening of the Suez Canal.

1840   1860   1880

Emperor Meiji modernized Japan and was the first Japanese emperor to meet a European.

Today you can visit the **Imperial Palace** in Tokyo, Japan's capital city.

Queen Victoria ruled England and India.

Today you can travel through the **Suez Canal,** which connected her two kingdoms. The opera *Aida* was written for the opening of this canal.

227

Lesson 1

The Age of Ideas

VOCABULARY

theory p. 229

geocentric p. 229

heliocentric p. 229

vaccine p. 232

Enlightenment p. 232

READING SKILL

Make Inferences

Fill in the chart to show how the Age of Ideas influenced modern science.

Text Clues	What You Know	Inference

STANDARDS FOCUS

SOCIAL STUDIES Science, Technology, and Society

GEOGRAPHY Places and Regions

Scientific instruments belonging to Italian scientist Galileo in Florence, Italy

Essential Question

How did scientific discoveries change how Europeans looked at the world?

A A scientific revolution began in the 1500s in Europe.

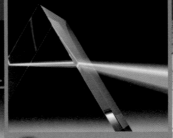

B Inventors created new instruments to test scientific theories.

C Doctors improved medicine with new ideas and methods.

A NEW UNDERSTANDING

In medieval Europe, Greek and Roman learning was mostly forgotten, but Arab scholars preserved it. Thus Europeans were later able to study the ancients and build on their knowledge.

After 1400, Europeans developed a process called the scientific method. In this method, scientists experiment to see if they can prove their ideas. An idea that is unproven is called a **theory**. Theories are proven by careful study of additional facts.

For example, Aristotle, the Greek philosopher, wrote that heavy objects would fall faster than lighter objects. Aristotle never tested his theory. According to one legend, the Italian scientist Galileo decided to test Aristotle's theory. Galileo is supposed to have dropped two objects of different weights from the Tower of Pisa in Italy. Both objects hit the ground at the same moment. Galileo had used the scientific method to prove that Aristotle was wrong!

Scientists began to question other ancient theories as well. Today we know that Earth travels around the sun. In the Middle Ages, people believed that Earth was the center of the universe. The belief that the sun and the stars revolve around Earth

is the **geocentric**, or Earth-centered, theory. A Polish scientist named Nicolaus Copernicus made a remarkable discovery in 1543.

> [I]n the middle of everything is the sun.
>
> COPERNICUS

Scientists proved Copernicus's **heliocentric**, or sun-centered, system by using mathematics. Soon, other theories were also being tested. Some were proven true. Others were shown to be false.

QUICK CHECK

Make Inferences **How did ancient Greece and Rome influence European science in the 1400s?**

◄ The bell tower of the cathedral of Pisa where Galileo supposedly tested his theory about gravity

B NEW INVENTIONS AND NEW IDEAS

The scientific method required new scientific instruments to test theories. As a result, thermometers and microscopes were developed. A Dutch inventor created the first telescope in 1608. Over time, improvements were made in eyeglasses, telescopes, and microscopes. Each year, it seemed, there were new ideas about the natural world.

GALILEO GALILEI

Italian Galileo Galilei improved the early telescope and studied the solar system. During his studies, he discovered four moons circling the planet Jupiter in 1610. His studies convinced him that the sun was the center of the solar system. As you have read, his discoveries led to trouble with Europe's rulers. Galileo wrote,

"[The universe] cannot be read until we have learnt the language . . . . It is written in mathematical language, and the letters are triangles, circles and other . . . figures . . . ."

Galileo's improved telescope ▶

JOHANNES KEPLER

Johannes Kepler was born in 1571 in Germany. He studied the work of other astronomers and improved the telescope. Using mathematics, he discovered that the orbit of Mars was an ellipse, or an oval. Kepler corrected the theory of Copernicus by stating that the orbit of the planets was elliptical.

Kepler discovered the way pictures can be made with a pinhole camera. He also studied the science of vision and correctly explained how eyeglasses work.

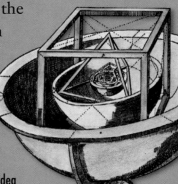

A model of Kepler's idea of the solar system ▶

Some of Europe's rulers worried about the discoveries. Church leaders, for example, put Galileo and his ideas on trial in 1633. Galileo agreed to say he was mistaken, although this was not what he truly thought.

QUICK CHECK

Make Inferences **How might scientists have influenced each other in this period?**

ISAAC NEWTON

An English mathematician, Isaac Newton studied chemistry and physics. He invented calculus, a new kind of mathematics. He used prisms to experiment with light. A prism breaks white light into the colors that make it up. Newton's studies also led to improvements in telescopes and other tools for astronomy.

Newton proved that a force pulled planets toward the sun. He called the force gravity. He developed an advanced form of mathematics to show how planets stay in orbit around the sun.

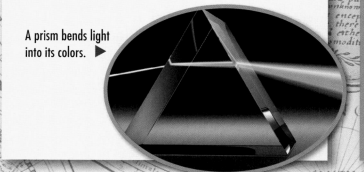

A prism bends light into its colors. ▶

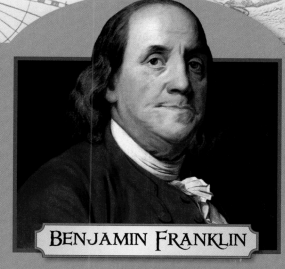

BENJAMIN FRANKLIN

The American Benjamin Franklin was a famous inventor and scientist. His inventions included3 lightning rods, bifocal glasses, swim fins, and the cast-iron stove. Franklin was respected by scientists in Europe.

Franklin correctly predicted that lightning was really a natural form of electricity. He may not have flown a kite in a storm to prove it, however, as the legend says he did. Several other scientists tried this experiment, and most were electrocuted. Franklin was perhaps the first person to understand the tremendous power of electricity.

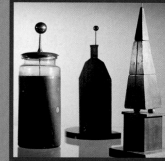

These lightning rod models were made by Benjamin Franklin. ▲

Ⓒ NEW IDEAS ADVANCE

18TH CENTURY INVENTIONS

YEAR	INVENTION	INVENTOR	NATIONALITY
1714	mercury thermometer	Daniel Gabriel Fahrenheit	German
1752	lightning rod	Benjamin Franklin	American
1753	scientific naming of plants and animals	Carl von Linné (Carolus Linneaus)	Swedish
1761	marine chronometer for measuring longitude	John Harrison	English
1775	discovery of oxygen in the atmosphere	Antoine and Marie Lavoisier	French
1783	hot-air balloon	Montgolfier brothers	French
1796	vaccine	Edward Jenner	English

Edward Jenner

Some important scientific discoveries are listed in the chart above. One was the smallpox **vaccine.** A vaccine is a way to build resistance to a disease. Edward Jenner noticed that people infected with cowpox, a mild form of smallpox, were immune from the disease. He used the first vaccine when he deliberately gave cowpox to a patient to protect him from smallpox.

The Enlightenment

The 1700s are called the **Enlightenment**, a period of learning or understanding. During this era, thinkers were excited about the new discoveries in science. They wanted to use reason just like the scientists had, but their goal was to improve society. They asked whether their governments and traditions were rational. Their questions prepared the way for major revolutions in America and France.

QUICK CHECK

Make Inferences **Why did Jenner vaccinate patients with cowpox?**

Check Understanding

1. **VOCABULARY** Write about some of the discoveries of the Age of Ideas using these vocabulary words.

   theory   heliocentric

   geocentric   vaccine

2. **READING SKILL Make Inferences** Use your completed chart to write about the influence of the Age of Ideas on modern science.

Text Clues	What You Know	Inference

3. **Write About It** Write a paragraph explaining how one invention in this lesson changed life in Europe.

   Essential Question

Chart and Graph Skills

Use a Climograph

VOCABULARY

climograph

A **climograph** is a type of graph that gives information about the climate of a place over a period of time. Climate is temperature and precipitation, or rainfall. Climate may be affected by elevation, by distance from the equator, or by nearby mountains or water.

Climographs can help you understand how people live in a particular place. For example, the amount of precipitation an area receives influences what types of crops farmers can grow. Changes in the amount of rainfall can affect farmers' harvests.

Learn It

● A climograph includes both a bar graph and a line graph. The bar graph shows average precipitation. The line graph shows the average temperature.

● Use the left side to read the bar graph. Use the right side to read the line graph.

Try It

● What was happening to the temperature during 1775 in London?

● How would you describe the precipitation in London during 1775?

● How would you describe the climate of London in 1775?

Apply It

● Make a climograph to show the average monthly temperature and precipitation in your community in the past year.

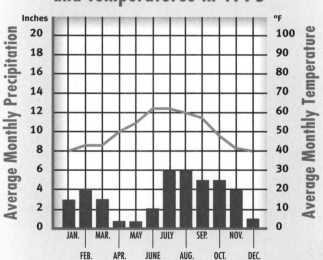

London, England, rainfall and temperatures in 1775

SOURCE: 16-59-1973 Manley (Q.J.R Meteorological Society, 1974)

233

Lesson 2

Exploring the World

VOCABULARY

caravel p. 235

circumnavigate p. 237

Northwest Passage
p. 238

READING SKILL

Make Inferences

Fill in the chart to show why European explorers wanted to reach Asia.

Text Clues	What You Know	Inference

STANDARDS FOCUS

SOCIAL STUDIES Global Connections

GEOGRAPHY Human Systems

In 1600, a Danish woodcarver created this scene of a geographer's studio.

Essential Question

How did Europe's sea explorations change the world?

A Europeans competed to find sea routes to Asia in the Age of Discovery.

B Columbus reached the Americas, and Magellan sailed around the Earth.

C Europeans looked for a water route across North America to the Far East.

EUROPEANS BEGIN TO EXPLORE

Europeans were willing to pay high prices for Asia's products. The profits of Asian trade inspired Europe's Age of Discovery.

In the 1400s, luxury goods from Asia were in great demand in Europe. It took luck—and several years—for merchants to travel across the Silk Road to reach Asian markets. Europeans began to search for another route to Asia.

Portugal Leads the Way

Henry the Navigator, a Portuguese prince, believed Asia could be reached by sea. Portugal is located on the Atlantic coast of Europe. Henry began sending expeditions in 1418. He established a school to train shipbuilders and sailors.

Each of Prince Henry's expeditions sailed a little farther south. Slowly, the Portuguese were able to extend the length of their voyages and map Africa's coastline.

The Portuguese improved the compass and the astrolabe, an instrument that helps pinpoint location. Portuguese shipbuilders also designed a new ship, called a **caravel**. Caravels combined the wide body of a European ship with the three-sided sail of Arab boats. The caravel was a sturdy ship that maneuvered easily in all winds.

In 1488, a Portuguese ship was the first to round Africa's southern tip. In 1502, Vasco da Gama became the first European to sail around Africa to India. Prince Henry's dream had come true.

QUICK CHECK

Make Inferences **Why did Prince Henry want Portuguese ships to reach Asia?**

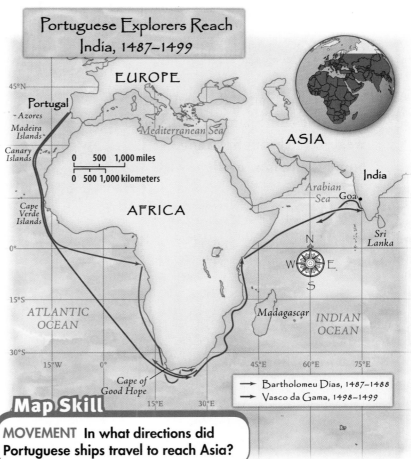

Portuguese Explorers Reach India, 1487–1499

→ Bartholomeu Dias, 1487–1488
→ Vasco da Gama, 1498–1499

Map Skill

MOVEMENT **In what directions did Portuguese ships travel to reach Asia?**

235

SAILING WEST TO GET EAST

Hoping to reach Asia, the Portuguese sailed down the African coast and headed east. Christopher Columbus had another idea—he would sail west to get to Asia. That meant he would have to cross an unknown ocean. When he set sail in 1492, he didn't know there were two continents in his path.

Across the Atlantic

On October 7, 1492, the crew spotted birds, a sign they were approaching land. Columbus thought that he had reached Asia, because he thought that Earth was about 10,000 miles smaller than it really is! He actually made landfall near the Bahamas.

His ships anchored at islands that are today Cuba and Hispaniola. Because he believed he was in the East Indies, Columbus called the native peoples "Indians."

Columbus sailed to the Americas four times for Spain, looking for wealth. He brought strange animals and new foods

back to Europe, but he found no gold. Spain's rulers lost interest in his voyages when there were no profits. Columbus died in 1506, never knowing he had reached two continents that we call the Americas.

Why *were* the new continents called America? In the early 1500s, an explorer named Amerigo Vespucci explored the coastline of South America. He had reports of his voyages printed. A German mapmaker read Vespucci's reports and named the new continents "Amerigo's Land," or America.

The caravel had space for cargo, sleeping quarters, and supplies of food and water for the sailors. ▶

food for crew

sleeping quarters

cargo

▲ This 1507 map by Martin Waldseemuller is the first map to label the Americas, named for Amerigo Vespucci.

First Around the World

By 1519, Europeans realized that the Americas blocked a straight westward voyage to Asia. In that year, five small ships set out from Spain. Their leader, Ferdinand Magellan, planned to sail around South America to reach Asia. Along South America's southern coast, Magellan and his crew faced the most dangerous seas they had ever seen. The Straits of Magellan, named for the explorer, are 334 miles of crashing waves and high winds. The tiny caravels plowed on until they reached calmer waters. A relieved Magellan called these waters the Pacific—or "peaceful"—Ocean.

Once he got around South America, Magellan thought he was close to Asia. In fact, his ships still had to cross 9,000 miles of ocean! Their food and water soon ran out, and his men had to boil their belts and shoes for food.

In 1521, Magellan's ships reached islands they named the Philippines to honor Spain's King Philip II. Magellan was killed and his crew faced a choice. Should they sail east or west to get home?

EVENT

Although he was killed by local people in the Philippines, **Ferdinand Magellan**, is remembered as the first person to sail completely around the world.

Ferdinand Magellan

In the end, one ship sailed in each direction. The ship sailing east was lost. The other ship continued to sail west and reached Spain in 1522. This little caravel, the *Victoria*, was the first ship to **circumnavigate**, or sail around, Earth. Magellan's expedition had lost all but 18 sailors and one ship. Yet the cargo of spices of the *Victoria* earned a tremendous profit. It was more than enough to pay for the entire expedition and all its losses. Europe's rulers now looked eagerly for new ways to reach the riches of Asia.

QUICK CHECK

Make Inferences Why would Magellan's crew have wanted to sail around Africa to reach Europe?

OTHER EXPLORERS SET OUT

European explorers believed there was a **Northwest Passage**, a water route across North America from the Atlantic to the Pacific. Of course, there was a passage north of Canada, but most of the time, it was too icy to be sailed.

European Explorers

Portugal and Spain were the early leaders in exploration. England was eager to compete for overseas trade and riches, too. So England's King Henry hired John Cabot, an Italian, to find a Northwest Passage. Cabot claimed what is now eastern Canada in 1496 for England. He discovered riches not in gold, but in some of the best fishing waters of the world—the Grand Banks off Canada's coast.

In 1524, the King of France sent an Italian, Giovanni Verrazano, to find a Northwest Passage. Verrazano was the first European to sail into what is now New York harbor. The Verrazano Narrows, a water passage in New York harbor, is named in honor of Verrazano.

Exploration cost money. Dutch merchants were the first to form stock companies to share expenses. In 1609, their company hired an English captain, Henry Hudson, to find a Northwest Passage. He failed to find a water route to Asia, but he did discover a broad river that still bears his name.

This reproduction of Henry Hudson's ship, the *Half Moon*, is docked on the Hudson River. ▼

QUICK CHECK

Make Inferences **Why might an Italian sail for England instead of Italy?**

Check Understanding

1. **VOCABULARY** Write a fictional diary entry of a sailor. Use these vocabulary words.

   caravel   **Northwest Passage**

   circumnavigate

2. **READING SKILL Make Inferences** Use your completed chart to explain why Europeans wanted to reach Asia.

Text Clues	What You Know	Inference

   Essential Question 3. **Write About It** Write about the influence of the expeditions of Columbus and Magellan on how Europeans thought of the world.

Map and Globe Skills

Use a Time Zone Map

VOCABULARY

time zones

Greenwich Mean Time

GMT

The voyages of discovery were long. You have read about how it could take years for a ship to return to its home port. Ships did not have regular schedules of arrival and departure.

Travel by train required a new system. Since 1884, the world has been divided into 24 **time zones**, one for each hour of the day. The Prime Meridian, which passes through Greenwich, England, starts the day. This time is called **Greenwich Mean Time** or **GMT**.

Learn It

● The map shows the world divided into time zones.

● To find the time in any region, look at the clocks. They show the time when it is noon at the Prime Meridian.

Try It

● What time is it in your time zone? How many hours are you from GMT?

Apply It

● Look at your classroom clock. What is the GMT when you read this page?

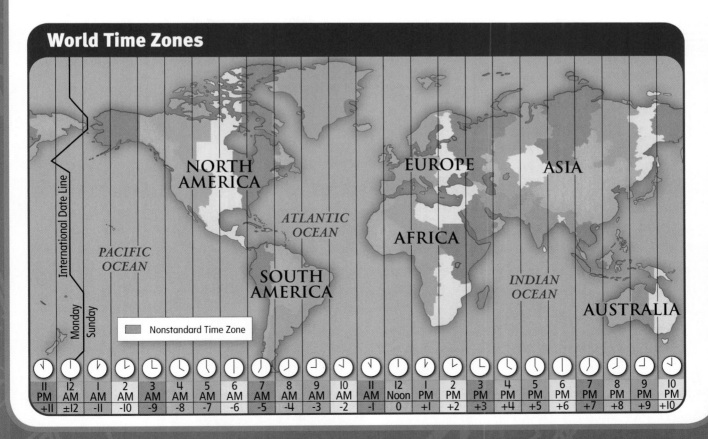

World Time Zones

Nonstandard Time Zone

| 11 PM +11 | 12 AM ±12 | 1 AM −11 | 2 AM −10 | 3 AM −9 | 4 AM −8 | 5 AM −7 | 6 AM −6 | 7 AM −5 | 8 AM −4 | 9 AM −3 | 10 AM −2 | 11 AM −1 | 12 Noon 0 | 1 PM +1 | 2 PM +2 | 3 PM +3 | 4 PM +4 | 5 PM +5 | 6 PM +6 | 7 PM +7 | 8 PM +8 | 9 PM +9 | 10 PM +10 |

Lesson 3

VOCABULARY

conquistador p. 242

immunity p. 243

triangular trade p. 246

Middle Passage p. 246

READING SKILL

Make Inferences

Fill in the chart with details about life after Europeans reached the Americas.

Text Clues	What You Know	Inference

STANDARDS FOCUS

SOCIAL STUDIES — Global Connections

GEOGRAPHY — Human Systems

EUROPEANS IN THE AMERICAS

Columbus and his sailors arrive in the Americas.

Essential Question

What happened when Europeans settled in the Americas?

 **A** Europeans argued about control of the Americas.

 **B** The Spanish defeated the Aztec and Inca empires and set up Spanish colonies.

 **C** Europeans enslaved Native Americans and Africans.

 **D** Triangular trade brought goods and slaves to the Americas.

240

A DIVIDING THE AMERICAS

By 1500, Spain was colonizing the Americas. Spanish soldiers quickly defeated the peoples of the Caribbean islands. Other European rulers began to look for wealth in the Americas.

Spain's rulers were concerned. Kings of Spain had paid for Columbus's voyage in 1492. Spain wanted to keep other Europeans from claiming lands in the Americas.

Spain was a Roman Catholic country, so Spain's rulers asked the pope to settle the issue. In 1493, the pope drew a north-south line down a map of the Western Hemisphere. He called it the Line of Demarcation. The pope gave all the land west of the line, which included most of the Americas, to Spain.

The issue of dividing the Americas was not settled by the Line of Demarcation, however. The pope's decision had little influence with Dutch and English explorers, since they were not Roman Catholics. Only eight years after Columbus sailed into the Caribbean Sea, the competition for colonies in the Americas had begun.

This Taino Native American figure shows a man playing a flute. ▶

There were people already in the Americas, of course, and they had lived there for centuries. Europeans ignored the rights of local peoples as they searched for new lands and followed rumors of gold.

QUICK CHECK

Make Inferences Why might the French, who were Roman Catholics, have ignored the Pope's division of the Americas?

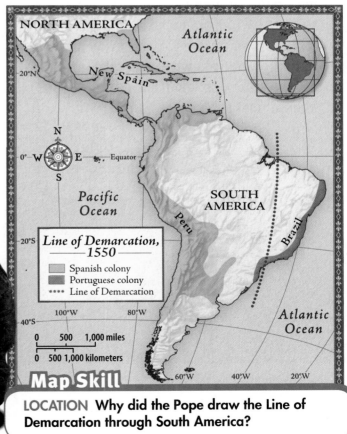

Line of Demarcation, 1550

- Spanish colony
- Portuguese colony
- •••• Line of Demarcation

Map Skill

LOCATION Why did the Pope draw the Line of Demarcation through South America?

241

Spanish steel weapons were stronger than Aztec clubs, but Aztec cotton armor was actually better for warfare in Mexico than the Spanish steel armor.

Primary Sources

...Moctezuma came to greet us and with him some two hundred lords, all barefoot and dressed in a different costume, but also very rich in their way.... When we met I dismounted and stepped forward to embrace him, but the two lords who were with him, stopped me with their hands so that I should not touch him....

Hernán Cortés to King Charles V, June 16, 1519

Write About It Write an eyewitness account from an Aztec point of view. Describe the meeting of Cortés and Moctezuma.

In order to establish colonies in South America, Spain needed to conquer the Aztec. In 1519, Hernán Cortés sailed with about 550 **conquistadors,** or conquerors, to Mexico. The Spanish were astonished by the magnificent Aztec capital, Tenochtitlan, but horrified by the Aztec practice of human sacrifice.

The Fall of the Aztec

At first, the Aztec did not attack the invading Spanish, perhaps because of an Aztec legend. This legend predicted that a blonde, blue-eyed god would appear about the time Cortés landed. Cortés happened to be blond. The Aztec might have thought that Cortés was this god of legend. In the Primary Sources box on the left, Cortés describes meeting the Aztec ruler, Moctezuma.

The Spanish conquest of the Aztec was helped by a Native American woman named Malinche, or Marina. Her skillful speeches convinced many Aztec enemies to join the Spanish. Also, the Spanish had exposed the Aztec to European diseases. The Aztec had no **immunity,** or resistance, to these diseases and thousands died. In August 1521, the Spanish captured Tenochtitlan, ending the Aztec Empire.

The Fall of the Inca

In 1532, conquistador Francisco Pizarro led an expedition against the Inca Empire in South America. Pizarro led only 185 men and 37 horses, but he had a plan to defeat the Incas.

The Inca ruler, Atahualpa, and 6,000 followers met the conquistadors at a town called Cajamarca. The Inca only had weapons of wood and stone. With muskets roaring and steel swords flashing in the sunlight, the conquistadors frightened Atahualpa's followers and captured the Inca ruler in the confusion.

To buy his freedom, Atahualpa promised to fill several large rooms with silver and gold. The Inca completed the task in eight months. Atahualpa's ransom today would be worth at least 250 million dollars! Even this fabulous treasure failed to save the Inca ruler. Pizarro broke his word and had Atahualpa murdered.

After Atahualpa's death, the Inca had trouble resisting the Spanish. As had happened with the Aztec, European diseases had killed many Inca. The Spanish extended their empire across South America.

QUICK CHECK

Make Inferences **Why might Pizarro have wanted to capture the Inca ruler?**

DataGraphic

Inflation in Spain

So much gold was shipped to Spain between 1500 and 1750 that gold began to lose its value. This caused inflation. Workers were paid more, but each coin was worth less. Answer the question about inflation in Spain.

Daily Wages (in grams of silver) in Valencia, Spain, 1500-1750

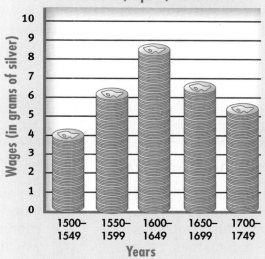

Real Value of Wages in Valencia, Spain, 1500-1750

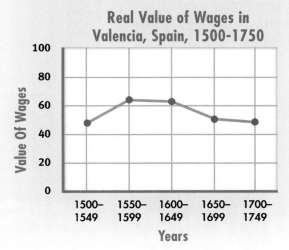

Talk About It Why were workers unable to buy as much after 1650?

© EUROPEANS COLONIZE THE AMERICAS

When Columbus returned to Spain, he brought unknown plants and animals to Europe. The Europeans, too, brought many new items to the Americas. This exchange of products is called the Columbian Exchange because it began with Columbus's voyages.

Enslaving Native Americans

In the 1500s, the Spanish government created *encomiendas*, or large grants of lands, to Spanish colonists. These grants also included all the Native Americans living on those lands. Spanish landholders had the power to force Native Americans to work for them.

In return for their labor, native workers were supposed to be given land to farm. They were also supposed to be protected and given instruction in the Christian faith. However, the *encomienda* system became slavery. Thousands of Native Americans died from disease, overwork, and punishment.

This cruelty angered some Spaniards. Bartolomé de las Casas was a missionary who worked to convert Native Americans to the Christian faith. Las Casas wrote to the king of Spain describing the terrible lives of Native Americans under Spanish rule. As a result,

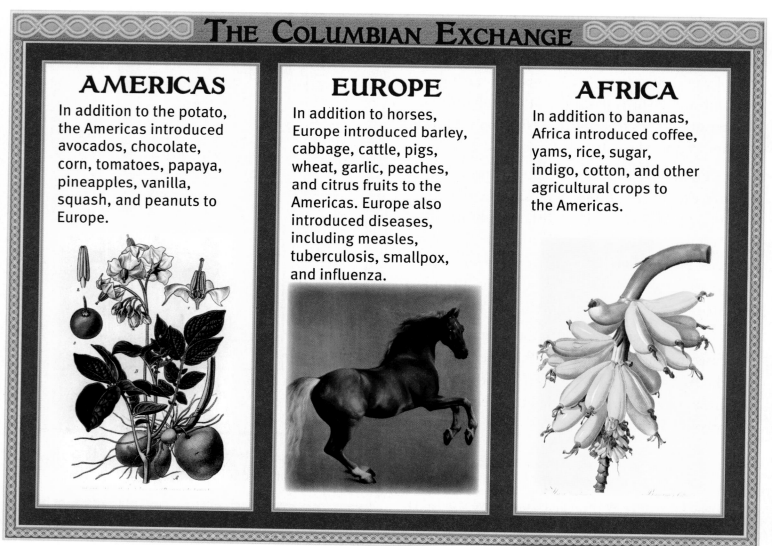

THE COLUMBIAN EXCHANGE

AMERICAS

In addition to the potato, the Americas introduced avocados, chocolate, corn, tomatoes, papaya, pineapples, vanilla, squash, and peanuts to Europe.

EUROPE

In addition to horses, Europe introduced barley, cabbage, cattle, pigs, wheat, garlic, peaches, and citrus fruits to the Americas. Europe also introduced diseases, including measles, tuberculosis, smallpox, and influenza.

AFRICA

In addition to bananas, Africa introduced coffee, yams, rice, sugar, indigo, cotton, and other agricultural crops to the Americas.

in 1542, new laws were proclaimed by the Spanish government. These laws were meant to protect Native Americans, but they ended up having a terrible effect on Africans.

The Slave Trade

In 1518, Spain's king granted a license for 4,000 enslaved Africans to be brought to the Americas. The slave trade had begun. Africans replaced Native Americans in fields and mines. Far from home, they were strangers trapped in a foreign land.

Usually, Arab and African traders bought or kidnapped Africans in Central and West Africa. The captives were then marched to cities on the Atlantic coast. There, they were traded for European goods or sold to European slave traders and loaded onto ships.

Conditions on slave ships were terrible. Men and women were crowded together for weeks below deck. "The shrieks of the women, and the groans of the dying, rendered the whole a scene of horror. . . ." one enslaved African recalled. More than one in ten Africans died during a voyage.

QUICK CHECK

Make Inferences **Why might Africans have had immunity to European diseases?**

Citizenship

Working for Justice

People like Bartolomé de las Casas fought against slavery. They wanted justice for all people. Today there are organizations that fight for social and economic justice as well. Some people give money to pay for lawyers for poor people or to fight discrimination. You may have heard of some of these organizations in your community.

 **Write About It** Write a paragraph telling what the word justice means to you.

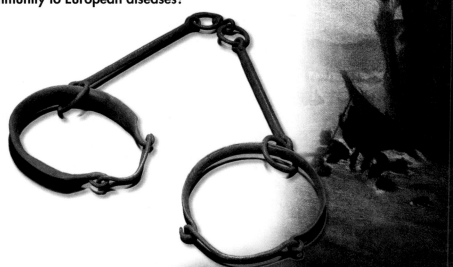

▲ Some Africans chose death by drowning (above) rather than a life of slavery. Others were fastened into iron collars (left) to prevent escape.

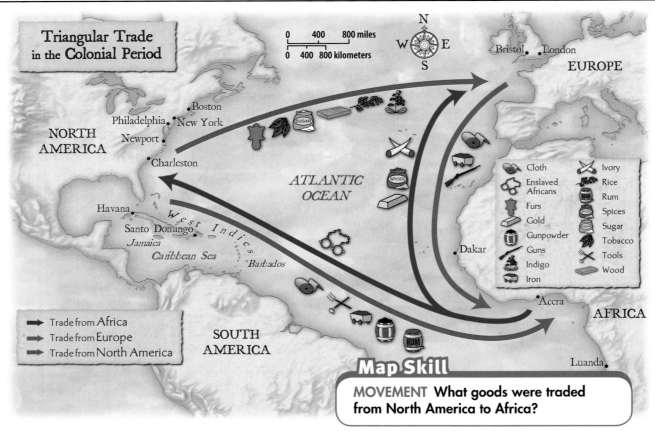

Triangular Trade in the Colonial Period

NORTH AMERICA

Boston
Philadelphia New York
Newport
Charleston

Havana
Santo Domingo
Jamaica
Caribbean Sea
Barbados
West Indies

SOUTH AMERICA

ATLANTIC OCEAN

Bristol London
EUROPE

Dakar
Accra AFRICA
Luanda

Cloth
Enslaved Africans
Furs
Gold
Gunpowder
Guns
Indigo
Iron
Ivory
Rice
Rum
Spices
Sugar
Tobacco
Tools
Wood

→ Trade from Africa
→ Trade from Europe
→ Trade from North America

0   400   800 miles
0   400 800 kilometers

Map Skill

MOVEMENT **What goods were traded from North America to Africa?**

In the 1500s and 1600s, merchants established trade routes across the Atlantic Ocean to transport goods.

Triangular Trade

As you can see on the map above, trade routes between Europe, Africa, and the Americas formed a triangle. These routes were called the **triangular trade**. In Africa, European merchants traded guns, cloth, and iron for enslaved Africans. Then, ships carried enslaved Africans to the Americas. This journey across the Atlantic to the Americas became known as the **Middle Passage**, because it was the middle part of the triangular trade. After the Africans were sold in the Americas, merchants loaded their ships with agricultural products, such as sugar, and sailed for Europe.

Results of the Slave Trade

Between 1500 and 1800, some 10 to 12 million enslaved Africans were sent to the Americas. Early in this period, most ended up in the region that is now called Latin America. Latin America includes South America, Mexico, and Caribbean islands such as Cuba and Puerto Rico. Slavery did not end in some parts of Latin America until the 1880s.

British colonies in North America allowed slavery. About six percent of enslaved Africans were sold to these colonies. Providence and Newport, in Rhode Island, were centers of the slave trade. About 100,000 enslaved Africans probably passed through these ports. Most eventually worked at plantations in the Caribbean. Others were sold to planters in what became the southeastern United States.

Enslaved Africans eventually became the majority population in the southern colonies of Virginia and South Carolina. Many enslaved Africans in the South worked on tobacco, cotton, and indigo plantations. Some northern cities also had many enslaved Africans. By the late 1700s, for example, New York City had more enslaved Africans than any other North American city except Charleston, South Carolina. In the North, enslaved workers usually worked in shops or on small farms.

The thirteen American colonies won their independence from Great Britain in 1783 and became the United States. By then, the new state of Pennsylvania had already banned slavery. Other northern states followed Pennsylvania's example. The trans-Atlantic slave trade was not outlawed until 1808, however, and slavery did not end in the United States until 1865.

QUICK CHECK

Make Inferences Why were there no enslaved Africans in Great Britain's Canadian colonies?

Check Understanding

1. **VOCABULARY** Use these vocabulary words to write a summary of the lesson.

| conquistador | Middle Passage |
| immunity | triangular trade |

2. **READING SKILL Make Inferences** Use your chart from page 240 to explain how Europeans changed life in the Americas.

Text Clues	What You Know	Inference

Essential Question 3. **Write About It** Write about how the Columbian Exchange changed life in the Americas.

▼ Enslaved Africans work in sugarcane fields on a Caribbean island.

THE FIRST REVOLUTIONS

Lesson 4

VOCABULARY

divine right p. 249

boycott p. 250

Bastille p. 251

READING SKILL

Make Inferences
Use the chart to show reasons for the revolutions in this lesson.

Text Clues	What You Know	Inference

STANDARDS FOCUS

SOCIAL STUDIES Power, Authority, and Governance

GEOGRAPHY Human Systems

Volunteers re-enact a battle of the English civil war.

Essential Question

How did new ideas lead to changes in government?

A The English civil war forced English kings to respect the laws of Parliament.

B New ideas led to revolutions in the United States and France.

248

A REVOLUTION IN ENGLAND

New ideas about government and equality swept over Europe in the 1600s. These ideas would lead to war and revolution in England, the Americas, and France.

In the 1600s, Europe's kings were very powerful. They claimed to rule by **divine right**. They believed that God had chosen them to be kings and had given them the right to rule in any way they liked.

The English Civil War

In 1215, the English king had agreed to sign the Magna Carta. It said that the king should consult with his nobles and respect their rights as feudal lords. In the 1600s, however, King Charles I insisted that he ruled by divine right and did not need to consult his nobles. For example, he taxed his subjects without consulting the lords in Parliament, the English legislature.

Parliament sent King Charles the Petition of Right in 1628. This document reminded the king that only Parliament could create and collect taxes. Charles ignored the petition. The argument between the king and Parliament led to a civil war in 1642. In 1649, Charles was defeated, and England had no king until 1660. Parliament invited Charles II to rule, but only after he had agreed to obey the demands of Parliament. English kings never again ruled by divine right.

The Glorious Revolution

Charles II died in 1685. His brother, King James II, tried to rule by divine right, but Parliament forced James to flee to France. Parliament offered the English crown to James's daughter, Mary II, and her husband, William. She had to sign a new agreement, the English Bill of Rights, in 1689. This document said that in any disagreement between the king and Parliament, Parliament had the final say.

QUICK CHECK

Make Inferences Why did Charles I believe that he ruled by divine right?

England's Charles I believed that God had chosen him to be king. ▶

AMERICA AND FRANCE

In 1763, Great Britain gained the lands east of the Mississippi River by winning an expensive war with France. The British government wanted the thirteen American colonies to help pay off this debt. The government began to tax goods.

The colonists protested. They felt they were British citizens, not mere subjects of the kings. Since their colonial assemblies had not approved the taxes, the colonists said that the taxes were illegal. Until the taxes were ended, the colonists began a **boycott**, or refused to buy British goods. Soon, fighting began between the British and the colonists.

The Declaration of Independence

Colonial delegates met at the Second Continental Congress in 1775. They voted to create the Continental Army and chose George Washington to lead it. In 1776, members of the congress signed the Declaration of Independence. This document said that Great Britain had abused the colonists' rights, so the colonies could form their own government. The colonies separated from Great Britain and established the United States of America.

Independence was not easily won, but the colonists did have help from the French. The French were rivals of the British and were glad to help. After six years of war, the British surrendered. In 1783, they recognized the United States of America as an independent country.

Revolution in France

The French government had borrowed money to fight the American Revolution. By 1789, there was no money left to repay the loans. King Louis XVI called a meeting of the Estates-General, France's parliament.

The kingdom of France was divided into three "estates," or classes. The First Estate was the clergy of the Catholic Church. The Second Estate was the nobles of France. These two wealthy estates ran France, but they paid few taxes. The Third Estate included nearly 98

◀ King Louis XVI (left) was beheaded during the French Revolution. Queen Marie Antoinette (far left) and thousands of others were also publicly executed.

percent of the population. Most of the Third Estate was poor peasants. They paid most of the taxes but had no voice in government.

The leaders of the Third Estate were upset. It was unjust, they said, that they had no power when they paid the most taxes. They formed a National Assembly and demanded a constitution. Worried that the king would defeat them, the poor seized the **Bastille**, a royal prison in Paris. There, they found weapons to defend their rights.

The National Assembly wrote a document called the Declaration of the Rights of Man and the Citizen. It stated that all men were "born and remain free and equal." The phrase "Liberty! Equality! Fraternity [brotherhood]!" became the slogan of the French Revolution.

In 1792, France's governing body, the National Convention, ended the monarchy and established a republic. The National Convention then set up courts to place people opposed to their authority on trial. As a result, the king, the queen, and 40,000 others were executed during the "Reign of Terror."

Napoleon Bonaparte

In 1799, a brilliant general named Napoleon Bonaparte seized power in France. After defeating most European rulers, Napoleon made himself emperor in 1802.

Napoleon established public education and created the Napoleonic Code. This set of laws guaranteed religious freedom and gave men the right to vote. At the same time, it limited freedom of speech and the press.

Napoleon fought many wars. In 1815, Napoleon was defeated and

I found the crown of France lying in the gutter, and I picked it up with a sword.

—NAPOLEON

forced to leave France. The ideas of equality and liberty continued to inspire revolutions throughout the 1800s.

QUICK CHECK

Make Inferences How might the American Revolution have influenced the French Revolution?

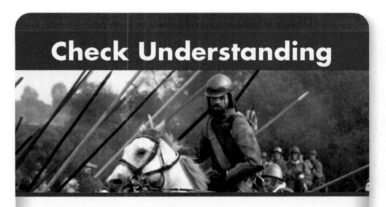

Check Understanding

1. **VOCABULARY** Use each vocabulary word below in a sentence that shows you understand its meaning in this lesson.

   boycott   Bastille

2. **READING SKILL Make Inferences** Use your chart from page 248 to explain how the English civil war might have led to the American Revolution.

Text Clues	What You Know	Inference

3. **Write About It** Write about why the colonists thought they had a right to vote on British taxes.

   Essential Question

Lesson 5

VOCABULARY

mestizo p. 254

confederation p. 256

READING SKILL

Make Inferences

Complete the chart to make inferences about revolutions in Mexico and South America.

Text Clues	What You Know	Inference

STANDARDS FOCUS

SOCIAL STUDIES Power, Authority, and Governance

GEOGRAPHY Human Systems

INDEPENDENCE SPREADS

Bolívar's troops attack the Spanish at a battle in Peru.

Essential Question

How did the idea of independence spread across the Americas?

A The American and French revolutions encouraged a revolution in Haiti.

B Hidalgo and Bolívar inspired Spanish colonies to fight for independence.

C Canada and Brazil peacefully reached independence.

Ⓐ REVOLUTION IN HAITI

People throughout the Americas heard about the success of the American Revolution. They also heard of the new French Republic. A desire for independence swept over the Americas.

The island of Hispaniola lies in the Caribbean Sea. In 1790, half of the island was ruled by France. French slaveholders sat in plantation houses and worried about the events of the French Revolution. They failed to notice the unrest in their own backyards. A revolt led by Toussaint L'Ouverture would drive the French out of Hispaniola forever.

Toussaint L'Ouverture

L'Ouverture had been enslaved. He gained his freedom and taught himself to read and write. In 1791, he led a slave revolt that drove out the French rulers. L'Ouverture took power and abolished slavery. He renamed the colony Haiti.

L'Ouverture was captured by French troops in 1802 and died in prison a year later. However, he remained a hero to the Haitians.

Haitian troops finally won independence for Haiti in 1804. Haiti became the second-oldest republic in the Western Hemisphere.

The Idea of Liberty

The revolutions in the United States, France, and Haiti aimed to achieve governments that represented all the people. Each revolution helped develop and spread the ideas of independence and equality around the world.

QUICK CHECK

Make Inferences **How did L'Ouverture inspire the Haitians to fight for freedom?**

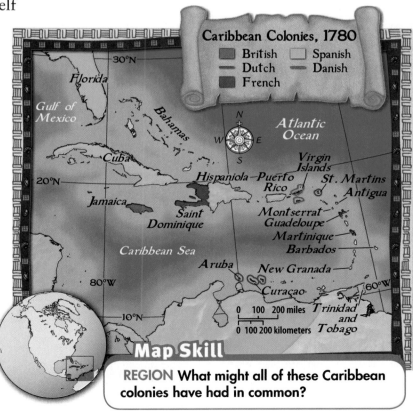

Caribbean Colonies, 1780
- British
- Spanish
- Dutch
- Danish
- French

Florida
Gulf of Mexico
Bahamas
30°N
Cuba
Atlantic Ocean
Jamaica
20°N
Hispaniola — Puerto Rico
Virgin Islands
St. Martins
Antigua
Saint Dominique
Montserrat
Guadeloupe
Martinique
Barbados
Caribbean Sea
Aruba
New Granada
80°W
Curaçao
60°W
10°N
Trinidad and Tobago

0 100 200 miles
0 100 200 kilometers

Map Skill

REGION What might all of these Caribbean colonies have had in common?

Ideas of independence spread to Mexico. Mexico was a colony of Spain, and all its government officials came from Spain. The wealth of Mexico went to Spain, while most Mexicans remained very poor. Many of the poor were **mestizos**. They had mixed Spanish and Native American ancestors. By 1800, many Mexicans had grown tired of foreign rule and wanted to control their own land and wealth.

The Cry of Dolores

Miguel Hidalgo was a poor priest in a town called Dolores in 1810. From his small church, Hidalgo preached that it was time for people to improve their own lives. One day, a large crowd gathered to hear Hidalgo speak. In his speech, which became known as the *Grito de Dolores*, or The Call of Dolores, Hidalgo demanded equality for all Mexicans. After his speech, the crowd left Dolores and marched toward Mexico City. Thousands of Mexicans armed only with tools and sticks joined the marchers. Their simple weapons were no match for trained Spanish troops, and the Mexicans were quickly defeated.

Events in Europe helped Mexico gain its independence. Napoleon Bonaparte took control of Spain in the early 1800s. Mexicans saw this weakening in Spanish authority as their opportunity to rebel against Spain. A Mexican army officer named Agustín de Iturbide took up the fight and won independence for Mexico in 1821. A year later, he declared himself emperor of Mexico.

Independence for South America

Other Spanish South American colonies took advantage of Spain's war with France. Two of South America's military leaders were Símon Bolívar and José de San Martín. The two men lived on opposite ends of the continent, but they shared a dream of independence.

Símon Bolívar came from a wealthy family in present-day Venezuela. He was well educated and had traveled to Europe, where he was inspired by the French Revolution. Bolívar dreamed of a United States of South America, made up of former Spanish colonies.

Bolívar began the fight in 1810. After nearly ten years of struggle, Bolívar defeated the Spanish in 1819. His followers created Greater Colombia, an alliance of Colombia, Venezuela, Ecuador, and Panama. Bolívar was named its first president. Then he turned his attention to the rest of South America.

While Bolívar's troops fought the Spanish in the north, a former Spanish soldier named José de San Martín fought Spanish troops in Chile and Argentina. First, San Martín freed his homeland, Argentina. Then he planned an attack to free Chile.

PEOPLE

Miguel Hidalgo was born in Mexico to Spanish parents. He spoke several languages and wrote books in the ancient Aztec language. Hidalgo was executed after he was captured by the Spanish.

Miguel Hidalgo

San Martín's plan was bold. He led his soldiers across the high, ice-covered passes of the Andes Mountains. The Spanish army in Chile was taken completely by surprise and was quickly defeated.

By 1822, the Spanish had lost all of their South American colonies except for what are today Peru and Bolivia. San Martín and Bolívar met to join forces, and then Bolívar led their combined armies in battle. The Spanish were defeated, and by 1824, there were no colonies under Spanish control in South America.

QUICK CHECK

Make Inferences **What might have inspired San Martín to fight for independence?**

◀ Símon Bolívar

Independence in South America

Map Skill

PLACE **Which two countries gained independence in 1822?**

José de San Martín and his troops across the Andes. ▶

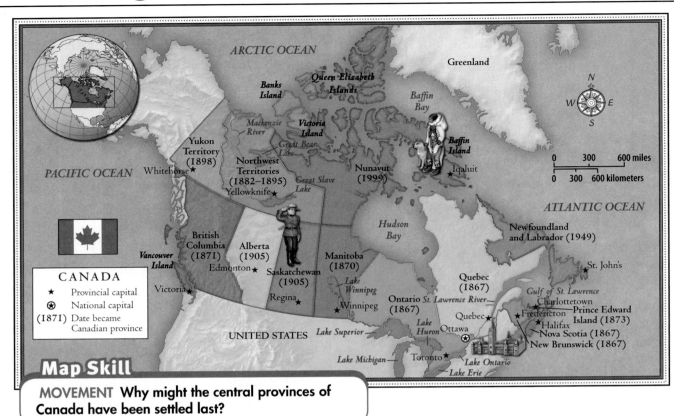

Map Skill

MOVEMENT Why might the central provinces of Canada have been settled last?

Gaining independence was not always violent. Two countries in the Americas, Canada and Brazil, reached independence without fighting or revolutions.

Canada in 1770

Canada was a French colony, but the British gained control of Canada in 1763. The British ruled each province, or state, separately.

The British government guaranteed the rights of French Canadians in 1774. This made them loyal to their British rulers, so they opposed the American Revolution. After the Revolution, thousands of Americans loyal to Britain fled from the United States to Canada. For many years, most of Canada's population was loyal to Britain and did not want independence.

Canada Unites

Over time, French Canadians began to resent British rule. In 1837, a rebellion broke out, and the British government realized that it would have to change the way it ruled Canada.

In 1838, Lord Durham came from London to study the situation in Canada. He recommended that the Canadian provinces be united. In 1867, Canada's leaders formed a **confederation**, an alliance of states that join together for a common purpose.

The king or queen of Great Britain remained the head of Canada's government. Canadians, however, took on more and more of the rights of an independent nation. Today Canadians celebrate July 1—the day their country became self-governing in 1867—as Canada Day.

Independence in Brazil

Brazil was a Portuguese colony. In 1807, King John VI of Portugal fled to Brazil to escape from Napoleon. He opened Brazil's ports to trade with all countries. He even issued a decree, or royal command, that made Brazil part of Portugal. The city of Rio de Janeiro became the capital of the Portuguese Empire.

After Napoleon's defeat, King John returned to Portugal. Before he left, he gave his son, Pedro, some advice. The king told Pedro that if Brazil declared its independence, Pedro should stay in Brazil and make himself the ruler of the new country. In 1822, Brazil did declare independence. Its ruler was the Emperor Pedro I. He was not a wise ruler, though, and was forced to leave Brazil in 1831.

Pedro's five-year-old son, Pedro II, became emperor. While he was a child, Pedro II had help ruling Brazil. As an adult, he proved to be

◀ Emperor Pedro II of Brazil

a far wiser ruler than his father had been. Pedro II ruled for more than 50 years and was a very popular emperor.

Under Pedro II, Brazil continued to allow slavery. The emperor did, however, take steps toward freeing the slaves. First, he freed children born to enslaved parents. Next, he freed enslaved workers over 60 years of age. His actions caused wealthy slaveholders to grumble in protest. Finally, in 1888 he signed a law ending all slavery in Brazil. Angry slaveholders rebelled and drove the emperor out. Brazil became a republic in 1889.

QUICK CHECK

Make Generalizations Why do you think that Canada and Brazil did not have violent revolutions?

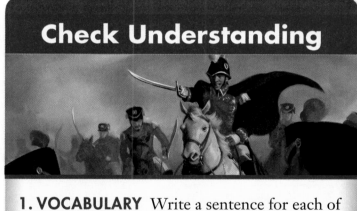

Check Understanding

1. **VOCABULARY** Write a sentence for each of the following words.

   mestizo   confederation

2. **READING SKILL Make Inferences** Use your chart from page 252 to explain the effects of revolutions in Latin America.

Text Clues	What You Know	Inference

3. **Write About It** Select one of the ideas of the American or French revolutions. Write a paragraph to show how this idea led to revolutions in South America.

   Essential Question

VOCABULARY

Industrial Revolution p. 259

factory p. 259

union p. 261

strike p. 261

READING SKILL

Make Inferences

Use this chart to make inferences about how the Industrial Revolution changed people's lives.

Text Clues	What You Know	Inference

STANDARDS FOCUS

SOCIAL STUDIES Production, Distribution, and Consumption

GEOGRAPHY Environment and Society

The Industrial Revolution

This factory in Berlin, Germany, made machines for other factories.

Essential Question How did the Industrial Revolution change how people lived and worked?

A As workers found jobs in new factories, towns and cities grew quickly.

B New technologies led to the growth of two new social classes.

258

A INDUSTRIALISM IN BRITAIN

In the late 1700s, another revolution began in Great Britain. This was not a revolution with armies, but a revolution in how goods were made. This Industrial Revolution was one of the most important in history.

Between 1750 and 1830, there was a change in how goods were produced in Europe. Instead of being made by hand, many goods were now manufactured, or made, with machines. This change radically affected the economy and also changed how and where people lived. We refer to changes in this time period as the **Industrial Revolution**.

For several reasons, the Industrial Revolution began in Great Britain. During the 1700s, Britain improved farming methods, producing more food. This led to a population increase. This larger population meant there were more workers and more people to buy goods. Great Britain had a rich supply of raw materials, especially coal and lead. These materials were needed in order to manufacture goods. People began to invest money into factories in hopes of making a profit.

Factories Change the Landscape

Huge machines were placed in a **factory**, a large building where workers gathered to manufacture products. Some workers left farms and settled

PLACES

The first cotton mill was opened at **Cromford, England**. Workers lived in nearby buildings. Today, the mill and its town are part of a national park in Great Britain.

Cromford cotton mill

near the factories. Soon small towns grew up. The towns continued to grow as more people came to work in the new factories.

Early factories relied on waterpower. Then, in 1769, James Watt invented the steam engine. It burned coal, which heated water and produced steam. By 1800, many steam engines were in use in Great Britain. This technology spread across Europe and to the United States.

QUICK CHECK

Make Inferences Why did the Industrial Revolution begin in Britain?

A model of James Watt's original steam engine of 1769 ▶

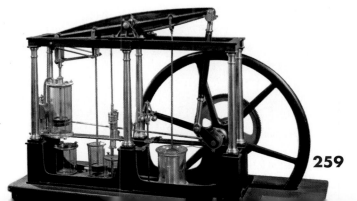

NEW INVENTIONS AND NEW CLASSES

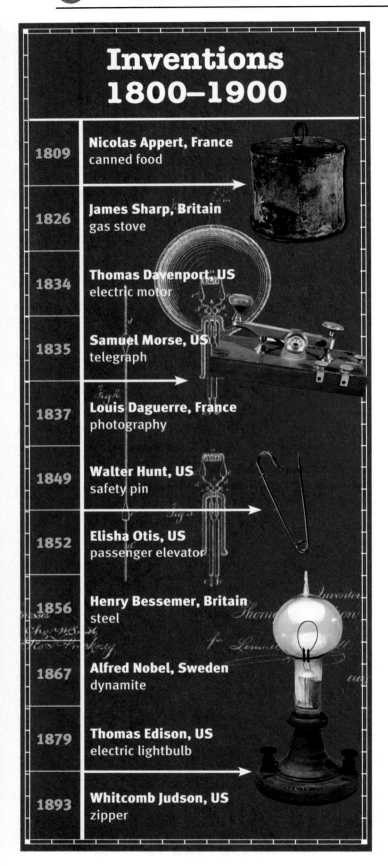

Inventions 1800–1900

1809	**Nicolas Appert, France** canned food
1826	**James Sharp, Britain** gas stove
1834	**Thomas Davenport, US** electric motor
1835	**Samuel Morse, US** telegraph
1837	**Louis Daguerre, France** photography
1849	**Walter Hunt, US** safety pin
1852	**Elisha Otis, US** passenger elevator
1856	**Henry Bessemer, Britain** steel
1867	**Alfred Nobel, Sweden** dynamite
1879	**Thomas Edison, US** electric lightbulb
1893	**Whitcomb Judson, US** zipper

James Watt's steam engine was one of the most important inventions of the Industrial Revolution. In 1807, Robert Fulton used the steam engine to power the *Clermont*, a steamboat, on the Hudson River. Around 1825, steam engines were used to move trains on iron rails. Soon railroads began to cross Europe and the United States. "The iron horse" moved people and goods quickly across large distances.

Technology on the Farm

Farmers also developed new inventions and techniques. Farmers learned to use fertilizers to make their fields more fertile. In 1831, Cyrus McCormick invented a mechanical reaper to harvest wheat. In 1837, John Deere designed the first American steel plow. This plow opened up farmland where tough prairie grasses had broken earlier plows.

The chart on this page lists some of the many inventions of the Industrial Revolution. As you can see, the 1800s were a time of great progress in technology.

The Development of Classes

The Industrial Revolution increased the power of two new social classes, the middle class and the working class. The middle class had always included bankers, lawyers, doctors, and merchants, but now it also included the new factory owners and inventors. One of the greatest changes of the Industrial Revolution was the growth in the power of the middle class.

The working class—factory workers in towns and cities—did not gain power right away. They worked 12 or 15 hours a day for low wages. They lived in crowded houses in the cities. Entire families had to work. Factory owners liked to hire children and women because they could pay them less than men.

Gradually, workers began to form unions. A **union** is a group of workers who unite to demand better working conditions. Unions threatened to go on **strike** if laws were not passed to improve their working conditions. While on strike, they refused to work until their demands were met.

The Industrial Revolution changed the way people lived and worked. In many ways, the Industrial Revolution began the path to the modern world we live in today.

QUICK CHECK

Make Inferences **How did the Industrial Revolution help to create the world you live in?**

Check Understanding

1. **VOCABULARY** Write a paragraph describing the Industrial Revolution. Use the vocabulary words in your paragraph.

   factory   union   strike

2. **READING SKILL Make Inferences** Use your chart to explain how the Industrial Revolution changed life on farms for better and for worse.

Text Clues	What You Know	Inference

   Essential Question

3. **Write About It** Why do you think that the 1800s was a period of so many inventions?

▲ Strikers march past a French ironworks in 1899.

Lesson 7

VOCABULARY

imperialism p. 263

nationalism p. 263

spheres of influence p. 266

READING SKILL

Make Inferences

Complete this chart with inferences about how imperialism changed people's lives.

Text Clues	What You Know	Inference

STANDARDS FOCUS

SOCIAL STUDIES Production, Distribution, and Consumption

GEOGRAPHY Human Systems

The Age of Imperialism

Europeans travel to Delhi for a meeting with India's mogul ruler, Akbar II, in 1815.

Essential Question Why did industrialized countries build colonial empires during the 1800s?

A European nations looked for colonies in Africa and Asia.

B Colonies in Asia provided resources and markets for European industries.

C Europeans controlled China, but Japan controlled its own trade.

D European countries colonized lands in Africa.

262

A   EUROPE EXPANDS ITS POWER

The products of the Industrial Revolution needed markets. European nations built empires to obtain raw materials and to provide markets for European products.

To keep their factories operating, industrialized European countries needed raw materials they could not find at home. They also needed new places to sell their manufactured goods. In the 1800s, Europeans set out to find these marketplaces and materials in order to expand their economies.

Empires Spread

Imperialism is the control of the economy and government of one country by another. Many countries have had imperial empires. For example, the American colonies were part of the British Empire in the 1600s and 1700s. The years between 1880 and 1914 are called the "Age of Imperialism," however, because during this time, European nations competed fiercely to establish colonies. They believed their industrial economies needed colonies. Great Britain had the largest empire.

Nationalism contributed to the fierce competition for colonies. Nationalism is intense feelings of devotion to one's own nation. This idea often led people to feel their nation was superior to other nations. In Europe, nationalism made some countries believe that their empires would improve the lives of the people they ruled.

QUICK CHECK

Make Inferences **How do you think the people of the colonies felt about the spread of European empires?**

European leaders met to decide how they would divide up the world into European empires. ▼

263

B EUROPEANS IN ASIA

Asia was an attractive place for Europe's rulers and merchants. Asian spices, crops, and metals were very valuable in Europe. By 1900, almost all of Asia was controlled or ruled directly by a European power.

India

You may remember that Lord Charles Cornwallis was the British general who surrendered to George Washington at Yorktown. The same Lord Cornwallis became the British governor of India in 1786. At that time, Britain controlled only small areas of India. Lord Cornwallis and later governors gradually expanded British control in India. Over the next 30 years, Great Britain continued to acquire new lands and more than 300 million Indian subjects.

The British ruled through the British East India Company. The company used Indian soldiers called sepoys to enforce their rule. In 1857, Indian sepoys revolted against British authority. The revolt was popular with Indians and spread quickly. Although the revolt was eventually put down by the British, confidence in the British East India Company ended.

In 1858, the British Parliament took direct control of India. Over time, British officials took control of India's economy and government. The British referred to India as "the jewel in the crown," their most precious

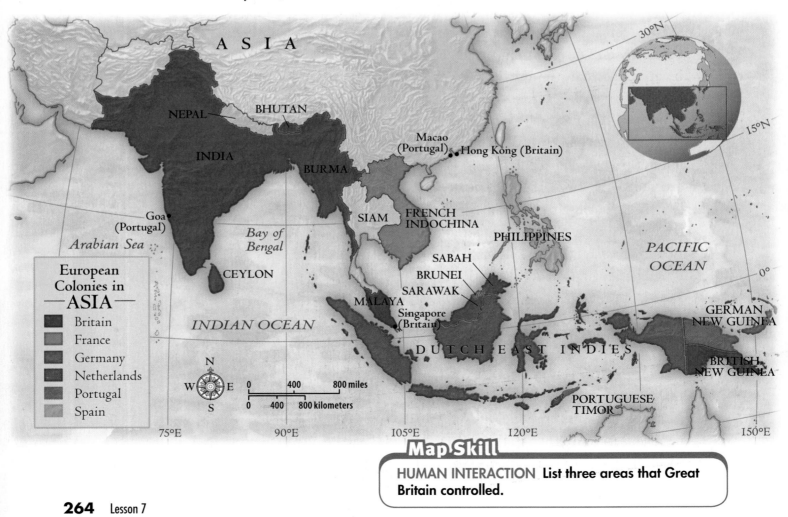

ASIA

NEPAL   BHUTAN

Macao (Portugal)   Hong Kong (Britain)

INDIA   BURMA

Goa (Portugal)   SIAM   FRENCH INDOCHINA

Arabian Sea   Bay of Bengal   PHILIPPINES   PACIFIC OCEAN

CEYLON   SABAH
BRUNEI
SARAWAK
MALAYA   GERMAN NEW GUINEA

European Colonies in ASIA

- Britain
- France
- Germany
- Netherlands
- Portugal
- Spain

INDIAN OCEAN   Singapore (Britain)   DUTCH EAST INDIES   BRITISH NEW GUINEA

N W E S

| 0 | 400 | 800 miles |
| 0 | 400 | 800 kilometers |

PORTUGUESE TIMOR

75°E   90°E   105°E   120°E   150°E

30°N   15°N   0°

Map Skill

HUMAN INTERACTION **List three areas that Great Britain controlled.**

▲ British troops battle with Indians during one of the wars making India a colony.

possession. However, the Indian people were not pleased with their British rulers. British rule destroyed many Indian crafts, because the British wanted India to be a market only for British products. British rule did, however, improve communications, transportation, and education. The British also built factories, railroads, hospitals, schools, and roads in India.

Southeast Asia

You have read how Europeans established colonies in Southeast Asia. The Dutch claimed a chain of islands, which are today the nation of Indonesia. This colony, called the Dutch East Indies, produced crops such as coffee, pepper, cinnamon, sugar, indigo, and tea. Mines provided tin and copper. Forests supplied teak, ebony, and other hardwoods. The Dutch used forced labor to collect these products. The Spanish did the same thing on their tobacco and sugar plantations in the Philippine Islands.

Beginning in the 1860s, the French established colonies in present-day Laos, Cambodia, and Vietnam. The French formed plantations to grow crops to export back to Europe. Although the French built roads, railways, telegraph systems, and schools, Southeast Asians had no voice in their own government.

In addition to India, the British took control of present-day Myanmar (Burma) in the early 1800s. They also extended their rule into Malaysia and Brunei. These lands had valuable resources and access to the South China Sea and the Indian Ocean. Among their colonies was an island called Singapore, which became an important port for trade in the region.

QUICK CHECK

Summarize Why were European nations interested in establishing colonial empires?

C CHINA AND JAPAN

During the years of European imperialism, China grew weaker. Europeans were able to divide China into **spheres of influence**, or areas that they controlled. Some European nations claimed parts of China as colonies.

Emperors Lose Power

Again and again, European powers forced China's emperors to accept humiliating treaties. Many Chinese ports were taken over by European traders. Within their spheres, foreigners did not have to obey Chinese laws. The Chinese saw their emperor as a weak and useless figure who could not protect China.

The Chinese were angry. A secret society, known as the Fists of Righteous Harmony, attracted thousands of followers. Foreigners saw the Fists practicing martial arts and called them "Boxers." The Boxers believed that European bullets could not harm them. The Primary Sources box shows how the beliefs of China's rulers encouraged the Boxers.

In 1900, the Boxers attacked foreigners and the foreign embassies in Beijing. After a 55-day siege, foreign armies rescued the embassies. More humiliation would follow for China.

European soldiers capture the Chinese emperor's summer palace near Beijing during the Boxer Rebellion. ▼

Primary Sources

The various Powers cast upon us looks . . . to seize our innermost territories. Should the strong enemies become aggressive (warlike) and press us to consent to things we can never accept, we have no alternative but to rely upon the justice of our cause. . . . What is there to fear from any invader? . . . Let us not think about making peace.

Chinese Empress Ci Xi, 1900

▲ **Write About It** What is the empress encouraging the Chinese to do?

▲ This traditional-style print shows the Japanese view of the American warships in Edo Harbor.

Japan and the West

In about 1640, Japan closed its ports to foreigners because it feared that European influence would weaken the government's authority. Then, in 1853, the American government sent warships to Edo, now Tokyo, Japan, asking to trade with Japan. Afraid, the Japanese signed a treaty agreeing to reopen their ports.

Many Japanese were angry about this treaty. They forced the shogun, Japan's leader, to give up power, and in 1868, a group of samurai restored the emperor to power. He changed his name to Meiji, so this event is known as the Meiji Restoration.

The new government moved the capital from Kyoto to Tokyo and began to modernize Japan. In 1889, a parliament, called the Diet, was created. Japan reorganized its economic, legal, military, and educational systems to be more like the West.

The Meiji government encouraged the Japanese to adopt European customs. People began to wear Western clothing, and students left Japan to study in Europe and the United States. Foreign experts designed factories and schools.

Under the Meiji government, Japan developed a powerful army and navy. Japan conquered Korea in 1894 and the island of Taiwan in 1895. In 1905, Japan surprised the world by winning a war with Russia, a powerful country. Later, Japan attacked China and seized the mineral-rich province of Manchuria. In less than 50 years, Japan had become the first modern nation-state in Asia. The United States and European nations began to see Japan as an important power.

QUICK CHECK

Make Inferences **Why were Europeans surprised when Japan defeated Russia in 1905?**

D AFRICA IS COLONIZED

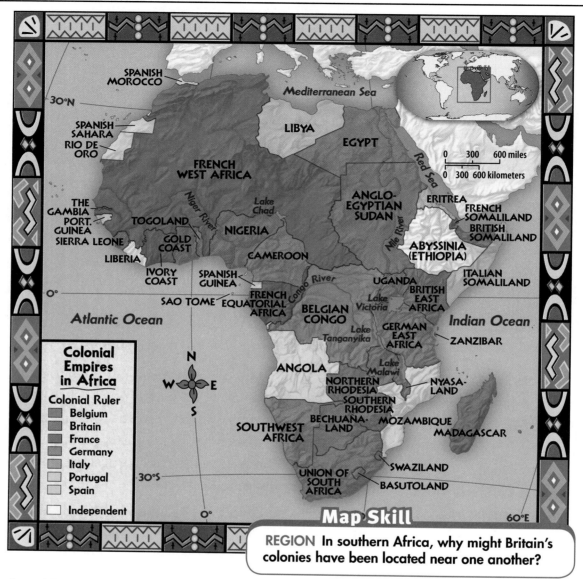

Map Skill

REGION In southern Africa, why might Britain's colonies have been located near one another?

In the late 1800s, European colonizers competed for control of Africa. This became know as the "Scramble for Africa."

Dividing Africa

Some European nations, including the Dutch, had long had trading posts in Africa, but most did not. In 1869, the French began to get involved with Egypt when a French company got permission to build the Suez Canal. The canal connected the Mediterranean Sea to the Red Sea, making it an important trade route. Great Britain used the canal to ship people and products to India. The British gradually gained influence over Egypt so that they could control the canal.

In Central Africa, European nations claimed lands for their empires. In the 1880s, King Leopold II of Belgium established a company to claim land along the Congo River. The company got African rulers to sign treaties for little money, and then the company enslaved local people to work on rubber plantations.

Other European nations, especially France, worried that they were losing out on profits in Africa. They began claiming land there, too. Some European companies treated Africans better than the Belgian king's company, but Africans still lost control of their own territory. By 1900, only Liberia and Ethiopia were still independent countries in Africa.

The End of Imperialism

Imperialism created many problems. Competition for colonies led to many arguments among European nations. People who lived in European colonies resented the rule of foreigners. Moreover, colonies were formed for the convenience of European governments. Colonial borders ignored Africa's history, traditions, and local cultures. This would lead to trouble later.

The year 1914 marked the end of the Age of Imperialism. European nations had succeeded in earning tremendous wealth from their colonies. But imperialism also caused friction among these nations. This friction increased nationalism, which contributed to the start of World War I.

QUICK CHECK

Make Inferences **How did the formation of European colonies affect Africans?**

Check Understanding

1. **VOCABULARY** Write a paragraph about European colonies using these vocabulary words.

   imperialism   **spheres of influence**

   nationalism

2. **READING SKILL Make Inferences** Use the chart to explain how colonial empires changed people's lives.

Text Clues	What You Know	Inference

   Essential Question 3. **Write About It** Explain why Europeans thought that imperialism was a good idea.

Africans carry a European supervisor in West Africa. ▼

Unit 5 — Review and Assess

Vocabulary

Write a sentence or more to answer each question.

1. Why was the geocentric view of the solar system incorrect?
2. Why did the Line of Demarcation not settle claim disputes?
3. Why did Europeans want to circumnavigate the globe?
4. How did the Industrial Revolution change life for people around the world?
5. Why did European nations practice imperialism?

Comprehension and Critical Thinking

6. Why did factory workers decide to form unions?
7. Why did European colonists bring Africans to the Americas?
8. Why did the people of France revolt against King Louis XVI?
9. **Reading Skill** How might Toussaint L'Ouverture have inspired other South American leaders?
10. **Critical Thinking** How did Japan change under the Meiji Restoration?

Skill

Read a Time Zone Map

Write a complete sentence to answer each question.

11. How many time zones are in the United States?
12. If it is noon in Washington, D.C., what time is it in Denver, Colorado?

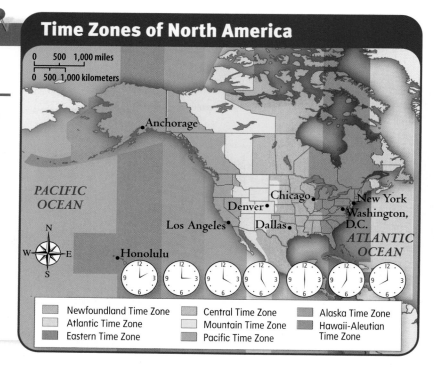

Time Zones of North America

Newfoundland Time Zone
Atlantic Time Zone
Eastern Time Zone
Central Time Zone
Mountain Time Zone
Pacific Time Zone
Alaska Time Zone
Hawaii-Aleutian Time Zone

 # Test Preparation

Study the climograph. Answer the questions.

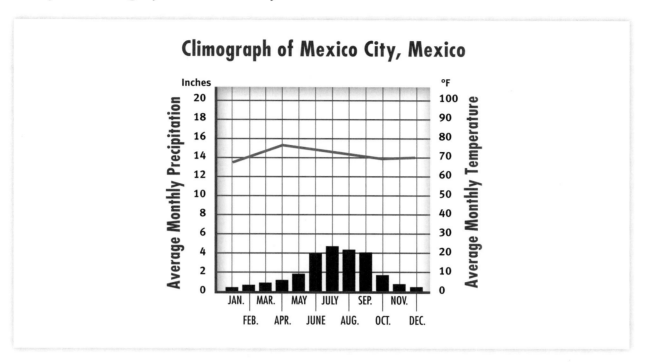

Climograph of Mexico City, Mexico

1. The purpose of this climograph is to show_____.

A. elevation of Mexico City

B. temperature in Mexico City

C. rainfall in Mexico City

D. climate of Mexico City

2. What is the average rainfall for Mexico City in July?

A. about 15 inches

B. a little over 4 inches

C. 75 inches

D. a little over 20 inches

3. What is the coldest month in Mexico City?

A. January

B. December

C. February

D. November

4. What effect do you think elevation has on the temperatures of Mexico City?

5. How might crops be affected if the climate around Mexico City got hotter and drier?

The Big Idea Activities

How do new ideas change people's lives?

Write About the Big Idea

Persuasive Essay
Use the Unit 5 foldable to write an essay about the Big Idea question.

Begin with an introduction in which you clearly state your opinion about changes caused by new ideas. Write one paragraph for each set of notes under a tab on your foldable. End with a concluding paragraph.

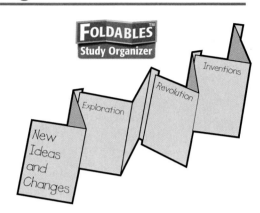

FOLDABLES™
Study Organizer

New Ideas and Changes
Exploration
Revolution
Inventions

Design a Poster

Work in small groups to create a poster announcing one of the new ideas in Unit 5. Your poster should have a colorful picture that illustrates the idea. You should also have phrases on the poster to tell readers why the idea is important.

1. Have one person design the picture for your poster.

2. Have one person write an exciting title for your poster.

3. Work as a group to come up with short phrases that explain why the idea is important.

When your group has completed its poster, display it in the classroom. Share your poster with your classmates. Explain why your group selected the idea and why your group thinks it is important.

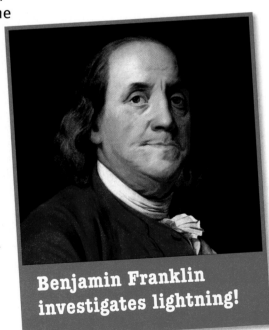

Benjamin Franklin investigates lightning!

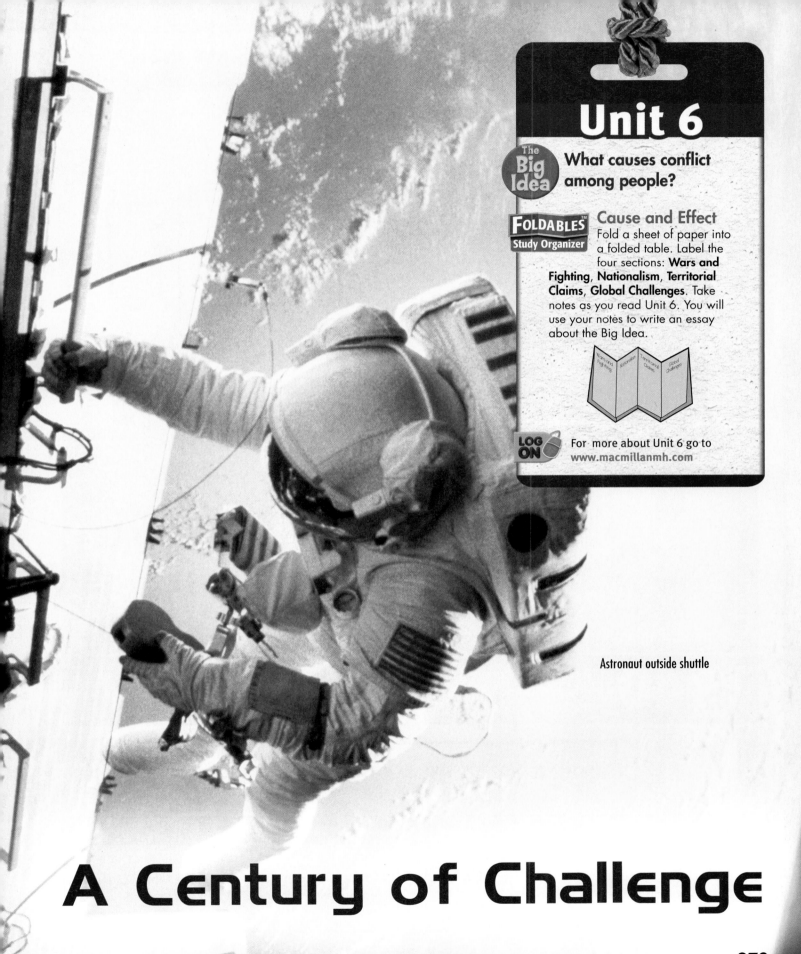

The Big Idea

What causes conflict among people?

FOLDABLES™ Study Organizer

Cause and Effect
Fold a sheet of paper into a folded table. Label the four sections: **Wars and Fighting, Nationalism, Territorial Claims, Global Challenges**. Take notes as you read Unit 6. You will use your notes to write an essay about the Big Idea.

LOG ON
For more about Unit 6 go to www.macmillanmh.com

Astronaut outside shuttle

A Century of Challenge

273

PEOPLE, PLACES, and EVENTS

Winston Churchill

Mohandas Gandhi

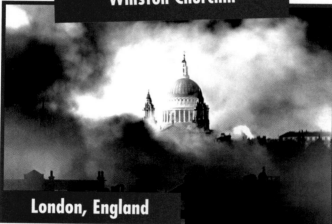

London, England

1940
German bombers attacked London during the Battle of Britain.

New Delhi, India

1947
Resistance to British rule grew in India during the 1930s and 1940s.

1940   1955   1970

Winston Churchill, Great Britain's World War II leader, led by example and delivered stirring speeches.

Today you can still see ruined buildings preserved as monuments to the Battle of Britain.

Mohandas Gandhi worked to peacefully end British rule in India.

Today you can visit **New Delhi**, where Gandhi led protests and strikes for India's freedom.

LOG ON

For more about People, Places, and Events, visit:
www.macmillanmh.com

Nelson Mandela

Michelle Bachelet

Capetown, South Africa

Presidential Palace, Santiago, Chile

1994

Africans led the South
African government for
the first time.

2006

Michelle Bachelet became
the first female president
in South American history.

1985   2000   2015

Nelson Mandela spent 28 years in prison for
his political activism. In 1990 he was released.

Today you can visit Pretoria, where he became
president of **South Africa** in 1994.

Michelle Bachelet was imprisoned during
Chile's dictatorship in the 1970s. She returned
after the dictatorship ended.

Today you can visit the **Presidential Palace**
in Santiago, Chile.

War and Revolution

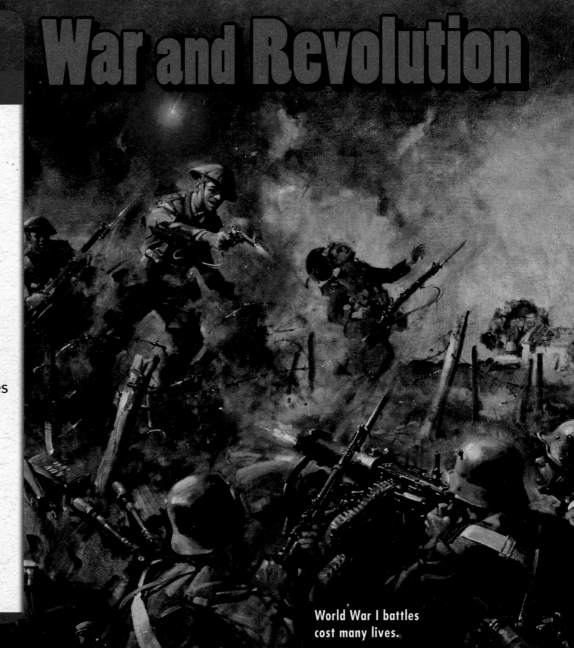

World War I battles cost many lives.

Lesson 1

VOCABULARY

alliance p. 277

armistice p. 279

communism p. 281

command economy p. 283

totalitarian p. 283

READING SKILL

Make Judgments

Complete the chart with details about the Russian Revolution. Use your notes to make a judgment.

Action	→	Judgment
	→	
	→	
	→	

STANDARDS FOCUS

SOCIAL STUDIES Power, Authority, and Governance

GEOGRAPHY Human Systems

Essential Question

How did political and economic change lead to conflict in Europe?

A European rivalries grew tense, and an assassination drove the continent into war.

B New technology made World War I deadlier than any previous conflict.

C Russia freed its serfs, setting off a series of events that led to a revolution.

D Under communist leaders, Russia's economy grew, but many people suffered.

A RIVALRY IN EUROPE

In the deep trenches of World War I, the soldiers' wet boots caused "trench foot," which made their feet swell to three times their normal size. Rats and lice also crawled over sleeping soldiers, spreading disease.

By 1910, many European nations were wealthy and powerful. Their factories produced much of the world's goods, and their armies patrolled their distant colonies. The future looked bright—but it was not.

Many Europeans had developed strong feelings of nationalism, which is extreme pride in one's country. Countries built up their armies to become more powerful than their neighbors. This weapons build-up made nations fearful of their rivals.

Governments began to make alliances with each other for protection. An **alliance** is a formal agreement to work together. In these alliances, countries promised to defend each other in case one was attacked.

A Murder Leads to War

The spark that set off World War I came on June 28, 1914. At the time, Austria and Hungary were one country. The government of Austria-Hungary controlled the neighboring region of Bosnia. Many Bosnians wanted to become part of the country of Serbia. On that bright, sunny June day, Archduke Franz Ferdinand of Austria-Hungary visited Bosnia's capital, Sarajevo.

The archduke and his wife toured the city in an open car. As they smiled and waved, a Serbian gunman fired twice, killing the archduke and his wife. Austria-Hungary's outraged leaders declared war on Serbia. So did their ally, Germany.

Serbia had powerful allies as well. Russia, France, and Britain all declared war on Austria-Hungary and Germany. By August, much of Europe was at war. As this happened, Britain's foreign secretary said, "The lights are going out all over Europe. We shall not see them lit again in our lifetime."

QUICK CHECK

Make Judgments What was a major cause of World War I?

Archduke Franz Ferdinand one hour before he was killed ▶

277

World War I

Central power
Neutral state
Allied power
✕ Battle

NORWAY
SWEDEN
North Sea
DENMARK
Baltic Sea
UNITED KINGDOM
NETHERLANDS
GERMANY
RUSSIA
BELGIUM
Somme
LUXEMBOURG
Verdun
ATLANTIC OCEAN
AUSTRIA-HUNGARY
SWITZERLAND
FRANCE
ROMANIA
Black Sea
SERBIA
BULGARIA
MONTENEGRO
PORTUGAL
SPAIN
ITALY
ALBANIA
GREECE
OTTOMAN EMPIRE
AFRICA
Mediterranean Sea

Map Skill

REGION Which nations made up the Central Powers?

▲ New technology changed warfare during World War I. Weapons like the machine gun and poison gas could kill hundreds of soldiers in trenches in a single attack.

B "THE GREAT WAR"

World War I, "The Great War," was different from previous wars. It involved almost every European country and many of their colonies. At the start of the war, European nations took sides. The Central Powers were Germany, Austria-Hungary, Bulgaria, and the Ottoman Empire. The major Allied Powers were Great Britain, France, and Russia. Spain and Switzerland were neutral, meaning they did not take sides.

In 1914, both sides expected the war to end quickly. It did not. By 1915, the Central Powers had entered France and Russia. The Allies, with more soldiers and supplies, stopped their enemies' advance, but could not push them back. Both sides dug long ditches, or trenches. In the trenches, soldiers crouched in the mud, waiting for the order to go "over the top" and attack.

In the Trenches

Trenches protected soldiers from the worst attacks, but living in them was miserable for soldiers. Trenches were wet and muddy in the winter, and hot and dusty in the summer.

In 1916, the Germans attacked the French at the fort of Verdun. The battle there lasted 11 months and killed nearly 700,000 soldiers. The Allies made their own great push against the Germans at the Somme River, in northern France. The two battles cost more than one million lives, but neither side gained more than a few yards of wet, soggy earth.

In all, more than 8.5 million people died during World War I. Millions more were wounded. With so many dead, people said that the war created a "lost generation."

Airplanes were used to spy on the enemy, drop bombs on their troops, and shoot down their planes. ▼

▲ The British invented armored tanks during World War I. New weapons introduced during the war made it more costly and more deadly than any previous conflict.

On the Home Front

World War I was the first "total war." Every citizen had a job to do. Young men became soldiers, while women, children, and the elderly helped on the "home front." They worked in factories or as nurses or ambulance drivers. They followed strict government limits on buying food and other crucial supplies. People ate less in order to feed soldiers in the trenches.

The United States Goes to War

When war broke out, the United States announced that it was neutral. But on May 7, 1915, a German submarine sank the British passenger ship *Lusitania*, killing more than 100 Americans who were on board. Later, in 1917, a secret offer was discovered: Germany had asked Mexico to fight against the United States.

These acts convinced Congress to declare war on Germany in April 1917. Within a year, almost two million U.S. soldiers were sent to Europe. With this support, the Allies won the war. On November 11, 1918, the Germans and the Allied Powers signed an armistice, or agreement to stop fighting.

A Troubled Peace

In June 1919, representatives of the opening sides met at the palace of Versailles near Paris, France. Germany was forced to sign a peace agreement known as the Treaty of Versailles. The harsh treaty angered Germans. It blamed their country for the war and demanded that it pay huge sums of money to repair the damage.

The treaty also called for countries to join a League of Nations, a group that would work to prevent wars by settling disagreements between nations. Although President Wilson liked the idea, Congress refused to join. An uneasy peace settled over Europe.

QUICK CHECK

Make Judgments **Was the Treaty of Versailles fair?**

THE RUSSIAN REVOLUTION

In 1900, life in Russia was not very different than it had been in the Middle Ages. The country was led by an absolute ruler called a tsar, the Russian word for emperor. Most Russians were serfs, or poor peasant farmers. In 1861, Tsar Alexander II had freed the serfs, but they remained poor and had few opportunities.

The First Revolt

The tsar lived in Russia's capital, St. Petersburg, a city of beautiful churches and palaces. The city also had terrible slums. Many poor peasants had moved to the capital looking for work. They lived in shabby, crowded neighborhoods, and worked long hours at any jobs they could find.

In 1905, workers started refusing to work in these terrible conditions any longer. They went on strike. On January 22, hundreds of peaceful strikers marched to the tsar's palace in St. Petersburg. The new tsar, Nicholas II, was not in the city, and his generals panicked and ordered troops to fire. More than 100 marchers were killed on "Bloody Sunday." Soon, workers across Russia joined the strikes.

As a response to the strikes, the tsar quickly set up a Russian parliament, called the Duma. However, he blocked every effort the Duma made to reform the government.

The Revolution Begins

Russia was still dealing with these crises when it was forced into World War I. But Russia was not ready for war. Its soldiers went into battle without guns or bullets, and more than a million of them were killed.

In March 1917, thousands of workers gathered in the streets of St. Petersburg. They shouted, "Down with the war," "Down with the tsar," and finally, just "Bread! Bread! Bread!"

Soldiers executed workers who protested in St. Petersburg in January 1905.

Vladimir Lenin speaking in Moscow in 1919 ▲

Soldiers were sent to the city to end the riot. They joined the protesters instead. The strike had become a revolution. When Tsar Nicholas II returned to the city, protesters stopped his train. He was forced to give up his crown. In July 1918, he and his family were killed. After 300 years, the rule of the tsars was over.

The Duma appointed leaders to serve until it could form a new government. They faced an almost impossible job—feeding the people, ending the strikes, and fighting World War I.

A New Kind of Government

Many Russians found hope in a political party called the Bolsheviks. It followed the ideas of the German thinker Karl Marx. Marx called his ideas socialism or **communism**. He said that workers should "rise up" and create new societies. All resources and businesses should be owned and managed by a communist government controlled by the workers.

The leader of Russia's Communist Party was Vladimir Lenin. During the war, he said he would seize private property and give it to the poor, so many poor Russian workers, peasants, and soldiers supported him.

In November 1917, factory workers, soldiers, sailors, and peasants helped the

Workers, unite! You have nothing to lose but your chains!

—KARL MARX

Communists take over the Duma. The temporary government, with only a few remaining supporters, turned over power without a fight. Once in power, Lenin began peace talks with Germany to get Russia out of the war. His party also took Russia's factories and farmland away from wealthy owners and put workers in charge.

QUICK CHECK

Make Judgments **How did freeing the serfs lead to major changes in Russia?**

Lenin made many enemies. He took land and factories away from their owners. He would not allow religious Russians to worship as they chose. He also demanded that ethnic groups across the large country give up their traditional ways of life.

Civil War in Russia

By 1918, Lenin's enemies and supporters were fighting a civil war. Millions died from battles, starvation, and disease. Finally, in 1920, Lenin's forces won, and Russia became the world's first communist nation. In 1922, it took a new name—the Union of Soviet Socialist Republics, or the Soviet Union. *Soviet* is a Russian term for a council of workers and soldiers. The government made Moscow its capital.

Lenin made dramatic changes. Along with seizing all factories, stores, and land, he closed all the churches in Russia. Factories were run by managers appointed by the government. Farmers had to give all their crops to the government. Food and other goods would be distributed to people by the government. In the middle of making all these changes, Lenin died in 1924.

◀ A 1934 Soviet poster, left, says, "Give first priority to gathering the Soviet harvest!" Below, women clean grain on a collective farm.

Stalin Takes Over

Josef Stalin a Communist leader, gained control of the Soviet government. Under Stalin, the government made all decisions about the Soviet economy. This is called a **command economy** because the government has total command over the economy.

Stalin forced all small family farms into huge collective farms, or large farms where everyone worked together. These collective farms produced grain and other crops for export rather than for the Russian people. Workers not needed on the farms were forced to work in mines and factories across the Soviet Union.

Under Stalin, the Soviet Union rapidly industrialized. Soviet factories produced more tractors than any other country in the world. Public schools were built for all children for the first time. Women had greater opportunities as well. But the Soviet people paid a high price for this progress.

The Soviet Dictator

Stalin's nation was a **totalitarian** state. The government controlled almost all public and private activity. It could also be a cruel state. Stalin ruled through terror. He ordered factory managers killed if they did not reach production goals. Those who complained were punished as "enemies of the state."

The number of these "enemies" reached into the millions. More than 15 million Soviet citizens were killed or forced into labor camps in the remote region of Siberia. The Soviet people did not get the "peace, land, and bread" that Lenin had promised. They did get more

▲ Josef Stalin

opportunities and a somewhat better standard of living. But they were not free.

QUICK CHECK

Make Judgments Why would the Communist Party want to close Russia's churches?

Check Understanding

1. **VOCABULARY** Use these vocabulary words in a paragraph about Stalin's government.

   command economy   **totalitarianism**

2. **READING STRATEGY Make Judgments** Use the chart from page 276 to explain how life changed for Russian farmers from the time of the tsars until Stalin's rule.

Action	→	Judgment
	→	
	→	
	→	

   Essential Question 3. **Write About It** How did conflict affect Russia after 1900?

Lesson 2

VOCABULARY

depression p. 285

propaganda p. 285

fascist p. 285

concentration camps p. 286

genocide p. 289

READING SKILL

Make Judgments
Complete the chart to make a judgment about people on the home front during Wold War II.

Action	→	Judgment
	→	
	→	
	→	

STANDARDS FOCUS

SOCIAL STUDIES Power, Authority, and Governance

GEOGRAPHY Environment and Society

WORLD WAR II

Allied troops ride through the wreckage of a French town after a 1944 battle.

Essential Question

How did the world change during World War II?

A In the 1930s, new governments in Italy and Germany began a new world war.

B German forces could not conquer Great Britain or the Soviet Union.

C As World War II approached its end in Europe, the Allies discovered the Holocaust.

D The Allies used the atom bomb, but later helped Japan and Germany rebuild.

A NEW DANGER IN EUROPE

The Treaty of Versailles, which ended World War I, forced Germany to pay huge fines for the damage caused by the war. This hurt the German economy. In 1923, an ex-soldier named Adolf Hitler demanded revenge.

In the 1930s, nations around the world, including Germany, suffered an economic **depression**. A depression is a time when many people are out of work and few people have the money to buy goods. One in three Germans had no job.

Germany and Italy

Adolf Hitler used **propaganda** to convince Germans that his Nazi Party would lead them out of the depression. Propaganda is the spreading of persuasive, but sometimes false, ideas to influence people. Hitler blamed Germany's problems on the Allies, communists, and especially Jews. He said that Jews were not loyal Germans. He said that the Germans were a "master race" that should rule the world. Hitler's ideas attracted many Germans. He took power in 1933, and boasted that the Nazis would rule for 1,000 years.

In 1922, Benito Mussolini had set up a **fascist** government in Italy. Fascist governments are totalitarian. They encourage nationalism, a strong military, a command economy, and, often, racism. Hitler's government was also fascist.

In 1936, Germany and Italy formed an alliance, and each began to seize new territory. Italy attacked Ethiopia, in Africa. Germany invaded Austria and Czechoslovakia. Other European nations watched the spread of fascism with horror. France and Great Britain were not ready to fight a new war, but knew they would have to act to stop Germany. Several countries signed a treaty agreeing to fight the Germans if they attacked Poland. In fact, that country was Hitler's next target.

QUICK CHECK

Make Judgments **Why did many Germans support Hitler?**

▲ Hitler, right, and Mussolini, second from left, review battle plans.

THE SECOND WORLD WAR

When Hitler's armies invaded Poland on September 1, 1939, France and Great Britain declared war on Germany. The Soviet Union did not declare war, because Hitler had signed a treaty with Josef Stalin promising not to attack the Soviet Union. Britain and France could do nothing to stop German troops from defeating Polish forces. Then, in 1940, Hitler sent troops into Belgium, Denmark, the Netherlands, and France. Germany conquered all of these countries quickly using its *blitzkrieg*, or "lightning war" strategy. France, a major military power, fell in just six weeks.

A major part of the Nazis' plans for Europe was to remove Jews from the continent. The Nazis and their supporters in the countries they conquered attacked and killed Jews and destroyed and stole their property. They also put millions of Jews into **concentration camps**— prisons where people are sent because of their religion, heritage, or political beliefs.

The Battle of Britain

By the end of 1940, after the fall of France, Great Britain was the last major European country still fighting Germany. Hitler believed the British government would surrender quickly if German planes bombed London and other important cities. He was wrong. Not only did the British refuse to surrender to the bombing, but the daring pilots of the country's Royal Air Force shot down more than 2,000 German planes in the skies over their country.

Still, night after night, for almost a year, German bombers flew over London. When Londoners heard the wail of air raid sirens, they rushed into subway tunnels for protection. Britain's king and queen refused to leave the city, even after their home, Buckingham Palace, was hit by bombs. Prime Minister Winston Churchill said,

> **"**We shall fight on the beaches, we shall fight on the landing grounds, we shall fight in the fields and in the streets, we shall fight in the hills; we shall never surrender.**"**

Royal Air Force pilots flew their Spitfires to defend Britain from German attacks.

Many people took cover in London subway stations during the Battle of Britain. ▶

More than 12,000 people died in the Battle of Britain, but the British never surrendered. Finally, Hitler stopped the attacks and turned to a new plan—an invasion of the Soviet Union. This terrible decision would be the beginning of the end for the Nazis, but it would still be four long years before the end came.

"The Great Patriotic War"

Stalin had signed a treaty with Hitler, so he did not expect a German attack. Hitler hated communism and the Soviets. After conquering Greece and Yugoslavia, German troops began an attack on the Soviet Union in June 1941. The Soviets, however, had a plan. They retreated from their cities before Nazi armies reached them and left nothing behind that could help the enemy. They even destroyed crops and factories. The people could not move everything, though, and Nazi troops looted and burned the old palaces of the tsars.

German troops marched to within 25 miles of Moscow, the Soviet capital, by November 1941. Then the weather changed. The temperature dropped below zero. Thousands of Nazi soldiers wearing summer uniforms froze to death. On December 6 the army began a retreat.

Still, Hitler would not give up his dream of conquering the Soviets. For two–and–half years, German troops surrounded the city of Leningrad (now St. Petersburg). No one could get out, and no food could get in. People ate wallpaper paste and boiled leather products into soup. More than a million people died, but, like the Londoners, they never surrendered.

In 1942, Nazi troops attacked the southern city of Stalingrad (now Volgograd). In a fierce battle during the frigid winter, Soviet troops stopped, then surrounded, German forces. Finally, after the deadliest battle in history, with more than 2 million deaths, the Nazis surrendered. The Battle of Stalingrad was a turning point of World War II, which Russians call "the Great Patriotic War."

QUICK CHECK

Summarize **How did the British and Soviets defend themselves against Germany?**

Smoke rose over London after a German air raid in 1940. ▼

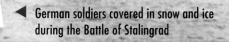

◄ German soldiers covered in snow and ice during the Battle of Stalingrad

The war in Asia began even before Germany invaded Poland. It started in 1931, when soldiers from the Japanese empire attacked Manchuria, a region north of China. By 1941, Japan had conquered Burma (now Myanmar), the Dutch East Indies (now Indonesia), almost a quarter of China, and hundreds of Pacific islands. Japan wanted to be a world power, but it needed the natural resources of the territories it conquered. Thousands died in the Japanese attacks.

Japan's victories, across the Pacific Ocean from California, worried American leaders.

At the same time, Japanese leaders feared that the United States might attack them in the Pacific. Japan decided to attack first.

Pearl Harbor

December 7, 1941, was a peaceful Sunday in Hawaii. The American naval base at Pearl Harbor was quiet in the soft morning sunshine. Suddenly the peace was shattered as Japan launched a surprise air attack on the base. The attack destroyed 19 ships, smashed 188 planes on the ground, and killed more than 2,200 people.

Americans were stunned. The next day, President Franklin Roosevelt asked Congress to declare war on Japan.

Americans rushed to get factories ready to make planes, trucks, and tanks for the Allies. U.S. troops soon joined the fighting in Europe and the Pacific. At home, Americans strictly limited their use of gas and collected iron and other scrap metal they could donate to the war effort.

◄ American battleships covered in smoke after the attack on Pearl Harbor

About 60,000 American, British, Canadian, French, and Polish soldiers died in the D-Day attack. Tens of thousands of Germans were also killed. Today visitors to **the beaches of Normandy** in northern France can see vast cemeteries dedicated to those who died in the fight to free Europe.

Normandy

▼ American troops landing on the beaches of Normandy

D-Day

After three long years, Allied armies had not been able to push Nazi armies out of North Africa or the Soviet Union. They decided to plan a surprise invasion of France to open up a third front, or battleground, in the war. The code name for the invasion was Operation Overlord.

On June 6, 1944, or "D-Day," 2,700 ships carried 200,000 Allied soldiers across the English Channel toward the beaches of Normandy, in northern France. Thousands of Allied soldiers died as they fought through German gunfire on the beaches. But the surprise attack worked, and the huge Allied force pushed back the Germans. Less than a year later, the Allies reached Germany. On April 30, 1945, Hitler killed himself, and a week later, Germany surrendered.

The Holocaust

As Allied troops marched toward Germany, they found the concentration camps where millions had been imprisoned or killed in Hitler's "Final Solution," or a form of genocide. A genocide is the planned

destruction of a racial, political, or cultural group. Jews, Roma (often called Gypsies), the disabled, and the Nazis' political opponents, worked as slaves, or were shot, starved, or gassed to death. Between nine and 12 million people died in the camps, including an estimated six million Jews. Before World War II, Europe had about 9.5 million Jews. By 1945, there were only 3.5 million. This crime is known as the Holocaust.

QUICK CHECK

Make Judgments Why was it important that the Allies open a new front in the war?

▲ Children trapped behind barbed wire

Germany and Italy had surrendered to the Allies by May 1945, but Japan fought on in Asia. In the last years of the war, European and American scientists had secretly developed a new weapon—the nuclear bomb. U.S. President Harry Truman knew the bombs would cause incredible destruction. He also knew that thousands would die if the Allies had to invade Japan. Truman decided to use the new weapon.

In August 1945, American planes dropped nuclear bombs on two Japanese cities, Hiroshima and Nagasaki. The cities were destroyed, and more than 100,000 Japanese were killed instantly. On August 14, Japan surrendered. After 50 million deaths, World War II was over.

The atomic explosion over the Japanese city of Nagasaki ▶

After the War

The victorious Allies did not punish Germany after World War II as they had done after World War I. Instead, they helped both Germany and Japan rebuild. In 1945, the Allies also led the movement to create the United Nations, to help countries avoid conflicts in the future. In spite of the wartime cooperation, the Allies themselves did not remain friendly with one another after the war. The Soviet Union would soon become a bitter enemy of the United States.

QUICK CHECK

Make Judgments **Why was it important to help Germany and Japan rebuild after World War II?**

Check Understanding

1. **VOCABULARY** Use these vocabulary words in a paragraph about the Holocaust.

   concentration camp   genocide

2. **READING SKILL** **Make Judgments** Use your chart from page 284 to show how people on the home front made a difference in the war.

Action	→	Judgment
→		
→		
→		

3. **Write About It** **Essential Question** Write a paragraph to explain why Germany started World War II.

Chart and Graph Skills

Use Picture Graphs

VOCABULARY

picture graph

A **picture graph** is a graph that uses pictures or symbols to represent large numbers of people or things. The picture graphs on this page show how many aircraft groups of countries produced during World War I and World War II. Follow the steps below to learn how to read picture graphs.

Learn It

- Read the title to learn the topic of the graph.

- The labels on the graph tell you how to understand the information.

Try It

Use the graphs to answer the questions.

- About how many aircraft were produced by the Central Powers during World War I?

- Which side produced more aircraft during World War II?

Apply It

Create a picture graph of your own, about the number of boys and girls in your class, for example, or the populations of different states or countries.

Aircraft in World War I

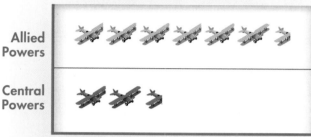

Each picture represents 25,000 aircraft

Aircraft in World War II

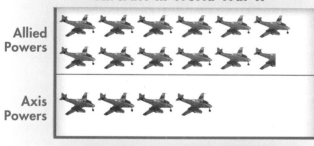

Each picture represents 50,000 aircraft

Modern China

VOCABULARY

Great Leap Forward p. 296

commune p.296

Cultural Revolution p. 297

READING SKILL

Make Judgments
Complete the chart to make a judgment about communism in China.

Action	→	Judgment
	→	
	→	
	→	

STANDARDS FOCUS

| SOCIAL STUDIES | Production, Distribution, and Consumption |
| GEOGRAPHY | The Uses of Geography |

A national flag show in Beijing in 2006

Essential Question

How did China become a Communist nation?

A Sun Yat-Sen led a revolution that ended the rule of the emperors in China.

B Mao Zedong's Communist Party gained control of China after a long civil war.

C Mao's policies led to the deaths and imprisonments of millions of Chinese.

D Today China has a growing economy, but the Communist Party remains in control.

A THE END OF DYNASTIES

Life in China had changed little over the centuries. In 1900 most Chinese were still poor farmers, and the emperors continued to rule from behind the walls of Beijing's Forbidden City. But all that was about to change.

In 1900, the Qing (Ching) dynasty ruled China. At first, they were strong rulers. Their power eventually declined. In the 1800s, and foreign countries began seizing Chinese territory. England took Hong Kong, and Japan invaded Taiwan. The Qing were too weak to stop the foreigners.

The First Revolt

Some people wanted a stronger, more democratic China. One of them was Sun Yat-Sen. As a young man, Sun had lived in Hawaii and in British Hong Kong. His travels gave him ideas about how China should change. Sun wanted the Chinese to have a voice in their government, and to regain their lost territories.

In 1911, Sun and his Nationalist Party led a revolution that ended the rule of the Qing. Sun became China's first president. The new republic faced serious problems. China was large, and the Nationalist army was weak. Local military leaders, or warlords, seized power in several regions.

The Nationalists turned to the Chinese Communist Party and the Soviet Union for military help.

These alliances helped the Nationalists keep control of the country.

Sun died in 1925, and his brother-in-law, Chiang Kai-Shek, became the leader of the Nationalists. Chiang did not trust his party's Communist allies. The Communists had, however, already won many supporters among the Chinese people. In 1927, the two parties—the Nationalists and the Communists—began a civil war for control of China.

QUICK CHECK

Make Judgments **Do you think Sun Yat-Sen's revolution was a success?**

Sun Yat-Sen ▼

293

COMMUNIST CHINA

By 1934, the civil war was going badly for the Communists. Nationalist troops had surrounded them in southern China, and cut them off from food and supplies. It appeared the war was about to end. Then the Communists made a daring escape. Communist leader Mao Zedong and 80,000 men and women broke through the Nationalist lines and fled to the north. Their escape, on foot, would eventually take them nearly 6,000 miles—almost the same distance as walking across the United States twice.

Their march was difficult, and food was often scarce. As one marcher later said:

❝We finished all our food, so we dug up wild grass and peeled the bark off trees. We even took off our belts and cooked them and added a little salt. And we survived.❞

◀ Mao Zedong

Nationalist planes and troops attacked the Communists as they marched. The Communists had to cross steep mountains and, in northen China, swamps and quicksand (watery sand in which objects sink quickly). The journey would become known as the Long March. Only one out of 10 people finished the march at Yenan, a city near the bend of the Huang He (Yellow River). The Communists found safety there and began to recruit new members.

The Long March

← Route of Long March

Beijing

Yenan

Huang (Yellow) River

35°N

Chang River

Nanjing

Luding

Chongqing

30°N

Ruijin

East China Sea

Kunming

25°N

0 200 400 miles
0 200 400 kilometers

115°E   120°E   20°N

Map Skill

MOVEMENT **In which directions did the Communists march?**

慶祝中華人民共和國國慶節

▲ A Chinese propaganda poster from 1950 shows people rejoicing at a national celebration.

World War II

China's misery increased when the country was attacked by Japan in 1937. Communists and Nationalists set aside their fight to join forces against the Japanese. As soon as Japan was defeated in 1945, China's civil war began again.

During World War II, Nationalist troops did most of the fighting against Japan. By 1945, many of their soldiers had died and their surviving troops were exhausted. The war also ruined China's economy. Hungry peasants were looking for change. The Communists promised them a bright new future, in exchange for their help fighting the Nationalists.

After two more years of war, the Chinese Communists forced the Nationalists into exile on the island of Taiwan, off China's eastern coast. Mao called his new Communist state the People's Republic of China. He told his supporters, "China has stood up!"

The Communists worked quickly to repair the damage caused by the war. They built new houses, sent doctors to the countryside, constructed new schools, and gave equal rights to women. They also took over all of the private land and businesses in the country. But many Chinese suffered during this period. The Communists killed more than a million people who objected to their policies. Many more Chinese would die in the years ahead.

QUICK CHECK

Make Judgments **How did World War II affect the outcome of China's civil war?**

C   A GREAT LEAP AND A FAMINE

A 1960 photo of a village's steel furnaces ▶

During the 1950s, China's economy grew, but slowly. Mao, however, was impatient. He wanted the country to grow faster and become a world power immediately. In 1957, he announced the **Great Leap Forward**, a plan to help China industrialize more quickly. The Chinese were ordered to work together to grow more crops and produce more goods. Workers were told, "More, faster, better, cheaper!"

Families were told to set up small steel furnaces in their backyards. They worked in the evenings to produce steel at home. These workers, however, had no training. Their steel was poor quality and could not be used.

Meanwhile, Mao ordered farmers to move into **communes** with as many as 20,000 other people. A commune is an organization where members share all resources, work, and living space. In the communes, people worked land owned by the government and planted crops the government demanded.

Life on the commune was completely different from the life most farmers had known. Men, women, and children slept in different buildings, and everyone ate together in large dining halls. The idea was to make people loyal to the government instead of to their families.

The Great Leap Forward was a disaster. Farmers resisted the orders of government officials who often knew nothing about farming. Farmers were often ordered to leave fields to build roads, bridges, and dams. Many of the communes' crops failed, and the failure led to massive famine. Almost 20 million people died in the famine.

The Cultural Revolution

In 1966, Mao began a new policy, designed to eliminate all opposition to communist rule. He called this shift toward a new culture the **Cultural Revolution**. Anyone who criticized the government, in any way, could be punished or jailed. Groups of young people called the Red Guard invaded people's homes and destroyed books about Confucius, traditional Chinese religion, or Western countries. They also destroyed collections of historic Chinese treasures. Clothing and style was strictly controlled, too. Anyone wearing "Western" clothes or sporting a Western-style haircut could be beaten.

During the Cultural Revolution, thousands of innocent people were sent to prison. Many of them were teachers, scholars, writers, and scientists. Mao said that these "enemies of the people" were American spies and traitors to China.

QUICK CHECK

Make Judgments Was the Great Leap Forward good for China?

Young Red Guards march through Beijing in 1971, holding Chairman Mao's "Little Red Book." ▶

QUOTATIONS FROM CHAIRMAN MAO TSE-TUNG

297

D   CHINA AFTER MAO

The terror of the Cultural Revolution continued until Mao's death in 1976, when Deng Xiaopang became China's new leader. Deng made some changes that helped China's economy grow. He allowed foreign companies to do business in China. He also let many farmers control their own farms again.

In the spring of 1989, college students gathered in Tiananmen Square in Beijing to demand that the Communist Party reform itself and become more open and democratic. Eventually, more than one million people joined the protests in the square and at other sites across the country. Deng, however, ordered Chinese army tanks into the square to end the protests. Hundreds of people were killed, ending the protests. Many Chinese were outraged that the government would use its troops against its own students.

In recent years, China's economy has grown rapidly. Today it is one of the largest economies in the world. Hong Kong, which Great Britain returned to Chinese control in 1997, has become one of the country's most successful territories. The Communist Party still tightly controls the country's government, however, and the Chinese people have limited freedom.

QUICK CHECK

Summarize **How has China changed since Mao's death?**

Check Understanding

1. VOCABULARY Use these vocabulary words in a paragraph about Mao Zedong's policies.

Great Leap Forward   **commune**
Cultural Revolution

2. READING SKILL Make Judgments Use your chart from page 292 to explain why Chinese farmers were upset about working on communal farms.

Action	→	Judgment
	→	
	→	
	→	

Essential Question

3. Write About It Why did many Chinese support the Communists during the country's civil war?

The modern skyline of Shanghai, a center of Chinese business ▼

Map and Globe Skills

Use a Cartogram

VOCABULARY

cartogram

A **cartogram** is a special kind of map that shows information rather than geographic features. Physical and political maps show countries as larger or smaller than their neighbors based on their actual size. A cartogram shows countries as larger or smaller than their neighbors based on information such as their populations or economies. Cartograms are useful for comparing information about several countries or an entire region. The cartogram on this page shows the size of the economies of nations in southern and eastern Asia. Follow the steps to learn more about using a cartogram.

Learn It

- A cartogram can compare countries based on any information that can be measured in numbers. The cartogram on this page compares the economies of southern and eastern Asian nations.

- Study the map title and the map key. What is being compared?

- In a cartogram, the size of a country tells you important information. Compare this cartogram to a political map of Asia. What differences do you see?

Try It

Use the cartogram on this page to answer the questions.

- Which country has the largest economy?

- Why is South Korea almost the same size as India?

Apply It

- Make a list of the kinds of information that could be shown on a cartogram.

- How else could you present the information from this cartogram?

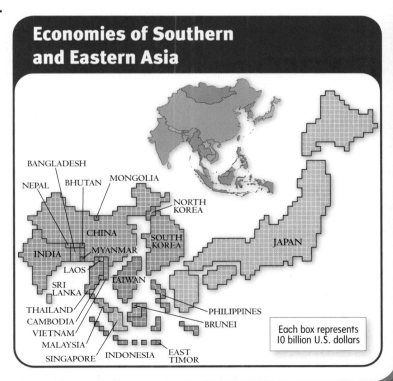

Economies of Southern and Eastern Asia

BANGLADESH
NEPAL
BHUTAN
MONGOLIA
NORTH KOREA
CHINA
SOUTH KOREA
JAPAN
INDIA
MYANMAR
LAOS
TAIWAN
SRI LANKA
THAILAND
CAMBODIA
VIETNAM
MALAYSIA
SINGAPORE
INDONESIA
EAST TIMOR
PHILIPPINES
BRUNEI

Each box represents 10 billion U.S. dollars

THE COLD WAR

READING SKILL

Make Judgments

Make a judgment about how the Cold War affected Americans.

Action → Judgment
→
→
→

STANDARDS FOCUS

SOCIAL STUDIES Time, Continuity, and Change

GEOGRAPHY The World in Spatial Terms

Winston Churchill, Franklin Roosevelt, and Josef Stalin at the Yalta Conference in 1945

Essential Question

How did the United States and the Soviet Union fight the Cold War?

A After World War II, the United States and the Soviet Union became bitter rivals.

B Two major Cold War conflicts were the Korean War and the struggle for Berlin.

C The world came to the brink of nuclear war during the Cuban Missile Crisis.

A A WORLDWIDE RIVALRY

Just before the end of World War II in 1945, the three major Allied leaders met in the Soviet city of Yalta to discuss how Europe would be divided up after Germany's defeat. When the war ended, things didn't go as planned.

The Soviet army had crossed into several Eastern European countries while fighting the Germans during World War II. Josef Stalin planned to put communist governments in charge of these countries to protect the Soviet Union in case another war began in Western Europe. Great Britain and the United States wanted each nation to be able to choose its own government.

At Yalta, Stalin agreed to remove his troops from the European countries under Soviet control. He feared the Americans and the British might order an attack on the Soviet Union while their troops were still in Europe. So Stalin broke the promises he made at Yalta. The countries of Eastern Europe stayed under Soviet control. This created what Winston Churchill of Great Britain called an "Iron Curtain" dividing the continent. Democratic nations were on one side. Soviet-controlled states were on the other.

At Yalta, the Allies agreed that each of them would control one

region of Germany after the war, but that the country would one day be reunited. The Soviets had other ideas. Stalin began his own plan for post-WWII Europe.

QUICK CHECK

Make Judgments What did Winston Churchill mean by the phrase "Iron Curtain"?

The Cold War
- Communist country
- Non-Communist country
- "Iron Curtain"

Map Skill

HUMAN INTERACTION **How could the "Iron Curtain" have affected people in Europe?**

301

B COLD WAR CONFLICTS

American soldiers in Korea, 1950

The United States and several Western European nations decided to prepare for the possibility of war with the Soviet Union. In 1949, they formed the North Atlantic Treaty Organization (**NATO**). NATO members promised to defend each other from attack by the Soviet Union. In 1955, the Soviet Union

created a similar alliance, the **Warsaw Pact**. The communist states in the pact agreed to defend each other in case of attack from the West.

The Superpowers

After World War II, the United States and the Soviet Union were the world's two "superpowers," or the nations with the most military strength. For almost 50 years

Koreans rushed to the south to find safety during the war. ▼

North and South Korea

0   100   200 miles
0   100   200 kilometers

RUSSIA

CHINA

NORTH KOREA

Pyongyang

Seoul

SOUTH KOREA

Yellow Sea

134°E

42°N

Sea of Japan

38°N   122°E

130°E

JAPAN

34°N

126°E

N W E S

after World War II, they struggled for power. Although they never fought each other directly, they were involved in smaller conflicts around the world. That is why the clash between the superpowers was called the "**Cold War.**"

The Korean War

The first armed conflict of the Cold War did not take place in Europe, but on the Korean peninsula. Korea had been divided into two countries at the end of World War II. North Korea was communist. South Korea was democratic. Each side wanted to reunite Korea under its own type of government.

In 1950, China helped North Korea invade South Korea. The United States and the United Nations sent thousands of soldiers to South Korea to try to defend it. The fighting went on for three years and caused nearly four million deaths. In 1953, troops finally retreated to the old border, and a tense peace began. Today, troops continue to guard this border.

Berlin Divided

The Soviet Union set up a communist government in its section of Germany—East Germany. The Allied-controlled regions of Germany united as a democracy—West Germany.

The capital of both countries, Berlin, was deep inside East Germany. That city was divided as well into East Berlin and West Berlin. In 1948, the Soviets tried to gain control of West Berlin by cutting off all land routes to it. West Berliners faced starvation.

The United States, Britain, and France began flying supplies into the city. The "Berlin Airlift" kept the city from starving. Finally the Soviets opened the roads and railroads again.

▲ The Berlin Wall split the city for nearly 30 years.

Many East Germans tried to escape to freedom by crossing into West Berlin. To stop them, East German police built the Berlin Wall in 1961. The wall split the city in two. It went through backyards, cut off streets, and smashed through buildings. Barbed wire, minefields, and floodlights guarded the wall. To get around it, some people dug tunnels or flew in balloons. More than 200 people died trying to cross to the West. The Berlin Wall stood until 1989, when East Germany's communist leaders allowed it to be torn down. Germany reunified, as a democracy, in 1990.

QUICK CHECK

Cause and Effect **How was the Korean War a part of the Cold War?**

C   TWO COLD WAR RACES

▲ After U.S. spy photos showed the Soviets building a missile base in Cuba, President Kennedy (far right) had to decide whether to go to war.

The Soviets saw the power of the atomic bomb in Japan and wanted the weapon for themselves. By 1949, Soviet scientists succeeded in building one. The superpowers continued to develop more powerful nuclear weapons throughout the Cold War. This competition to create the most powerful nuclear weapons, or the **arms race**, made many people around the world fear the possibility of a nuclear war. In the United States, families dug bomb shelters, and schoolchildren practiced what to do if the nation was attacked.

The superpowers also competed in a "**space race**." In 1957, the Soviets won an early victory in the race. They shocked the world by launching Sputnik, the first satellite, or human-made object, into Earth's orbit.

An American nuclear missile being tested in 1983 ▶

In 1962, President John F. Kennedy set a goal of landing an American astronaut on the moon by the end of the decade. The United States made the space race a national priority, and in 1969, Kennedy's challenge was met. On July 20 the world watched and cheered as astronaut Neil Armstrong became the first human to step onto the lunar surface. Edwin "Buzz" Aldrin later stepped onto the moon as well.

The astronauts placed an American flag on the lunar surface, as well as a plaque reading, "Here men from the planet Earth first set foot upon the Moon July 1969 AD. We came in peace for all mankind." Eventually, 12 astronauts would walk on the moon, the last ones in December 1972. No one has been to the moon since.

EVENT

As part of the Apollo 11 mission, two astronauts landed a spacecraft on the moon on July 20, 1969. **Neil Armstrong took the first steps onto the moon's surface**, saying, "That's one small step for man, one giant leap for mankind."

The Moon Landing

The Cuban Missile Crisis

The Cold War heated up again in October 1962. Communist Fidel Castro had led a revolt against Cuban dictator Fulgencio Batista and taken power in Cuba in 1959. The Soviet Union supported Castro's leadership and sent weapons to his government. Then in the summer of 1962, Soviet leader Nikita Khrushchev began sending nuclear missiles to Cuba. The new missile base in Cuba was just 90 miles from Florida.

President John F. Kennedy demanded that the Soviet Union remove the missiles, but Khrushchev refused. He said that since the United States had nuclear weapons in Turkey, which was next to the Soviet Union, the Soviets could place missiles in a country next to the United States.

On October 22, Kennedy told Americans about the Cuban missiles. Many Americans, and other people around the world, were afraid that the dispute might lead to a third world war, this one fought with nuclear weapons.

After several tense days, however, the superpowers reached an agreement on October 28. The Soviets would take their missiles out of Cuba, and the United States would remove its missiles from Turkey and from nearby Italy. The world breathed a sigh of relief.

Hopes for Peace

The Cuban missile crisis showed the leaders of both superpowers how risky the Cold War could be. After the crisis, a special telephone connection known as a "hotline" was set up between Moscow and Washington, D.C., so that the countries could communicate quickly during any future crisis. American and Soviet leaders spent the next 30 years trying to prevent nuclear weapons from spreading to other countries around the world.

QUICK CHECK

Make Judgments **Why didn't the Cuban missile crisis lead to war between the superpowers?**

Check Understanding

1. **VOCABULARY** Use these vocabulary words in a paragraph about the Cold War.

   NATO   arms race   space race

2. **READING SKILL Make Judgments** Use your chart from page 300 to explain how the Cold War affected Americans.

Action	→	Judgment
	→	
	→	
	→	

3. **Write About It** How were science and technology important parts of the Cold War?

Lesson 5

VOCABULARY

civil disobedience p. 307

Green Revolution p. 308

READING SKILL

Make Judgments
Complete the chart with details about independence in India. Use your notes to make a judgment.

Action	→	Judgment
	→	
	→	
	→	

STANDARDS FOCUS

SOCIAL STUDIES Power, Authority, and Governance

GEOGRAPHY Human Systems

STRUGGLES IN INDIA

Gandhi leads an independence march.

Essential Question

How did conflicts affect the development of modern South Asia?

A Gandhi organized protests and marches against British rule in India.

B South Asians have fought wars and struggled to join the global economy.

306

BRITISH RULE

Great Britain called India "the jewel in the crown." It was Great Britain's largest colony. British rulers seemed beyond challenge. A single man with a simple idea, however, won independence for India.

For almost 200 years, the British colony of India included the modern nations of Pakistan, Bangladesh, and Sri Lanka. The British controlled the Indian economy and used India as a market for English goods.

Indians Fight Back

In 1915, an Indian leader, Mohandas Gandhi, began to lead resistance to British rule. Because of Gandhi's simple life and deep faith, he earned the title Mahatma, or "great soul." Gandhi taught **civil disobedience**, or nonviolent refusal to follow the orders of a government. Indians refused to pay taxes, and they would not buy British products.

The British government suppressed these protests for decades. Nonviolence was sometimes met with British violence. However, the hard work and sacrifices of the Indian people paid off. They won their independence from Britain in 1947. Gandhi was not a political leader, so Jawaharlal Nehru rose up to fill that role.

Like Gandhi, Nehru and his supporters were Hindus. Muslims were afraid they would have no power in the new India. Under the leadership of Mohammed Ali Jinnah, the Muslim majority regions of India united into a Muslim nation in 1947. This new nation was called Pakistan.

Civil War Erupts

In 1947, Pakistan and India became independent nations. Within weeks, a bloody civil war broke out between them. Gandhi worked to bring the two nations together and went on a hunger strike until the fighting ended. A Hindu assassinated Gandhi in 1948 because he felt that Gandhi had hurt the Hindu cause.

QUICK CHECK

Make Judgments Why do you think Indians rebelled against British rule?

India leader Nehru (left) and Pakistani leader Jinnah (right) ▶

307

SOUTH ASIA TODAY

Independent Nations

At the time of independence, India was suffering from the worst famine in modern history. At least four million people starved to death. Raising food became the new nation's first goal. The government soon began to develop more productive crops. This program became known as the **Green Revolution**.

In the 1940s and 1950s, the Indian government granted women the right to own property and vote. India is one of the first countries to have a woman as its political leader. Nehru's daughter, Indira Gandhi, became India's prime minister in 1966.

In 1971, India and Pakistan went to war again. During the war, the eastern part of Pakistan declared independence and became the nation of Bangladesh.

The Modern Indian Economy

India is a country of economic extremes. While parts of the economy thrive, poverty is very widespread. Millions of people lack shelter and access to clean water.

Bombay, now called Mumbai, is the center of India's huge movie industry. More than twice as many movies are made in Bombay as in Hollywood. In fact, the city is nicknamed "Bollywood." Indian films usually have a huge cast that sings and dances through wonderful adventures. However, the film industry is only a small part of India's booming economy.

A High Tech Powerhouse

When you need advice about your computer or need to buy an airline ticket, you often call a central number. Frequently you will talk

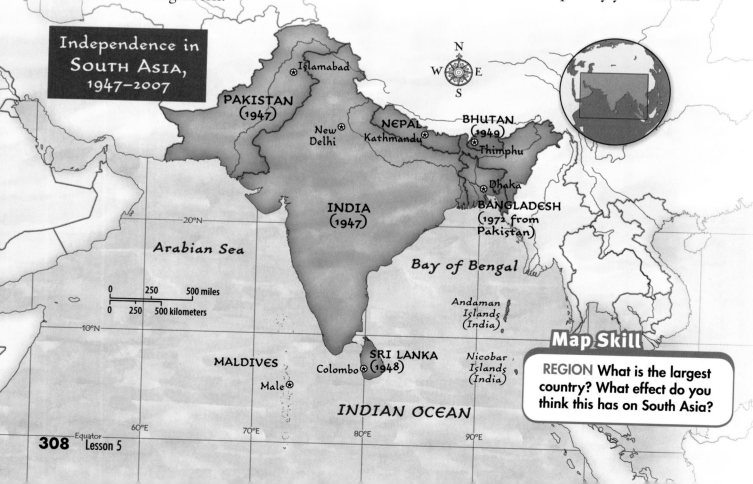

Independence in SOUTH ASIA, 1947–2007

Islamabad

PAKISTAN (1947)

New Delhi

NEPAL
Kathmandu

BHUTAN (1949)
Thimphu

Dhaka

BANGLADESH (1972 from Pakistan)

INDIA (1947)

20°N

Arabian Sea

Bay of Bengal

0   250   500 miles
0   250   500 kilometers

10°N

Andaman Islands (India)

MALDIVES

Colombo

SRI LANKA (1948)

Nicobar Islands (India)

Male

INDIAN OCEAN

60°E   70°E   80°E   90°E

Equator

N W E S

Map Skill

REGION What is the largest country? What effect do you think this has on South Asia?

▼ A director instructs an actor on an Indian film set.

▲ Women learn computer skills in Bengaluru, India.

to someone in India. That is because many American companies have phone centers in India. Because it was a British colony, many people in India speak English. Telephone centers have become big business.

India is also a center of high tech, short for "high technology." Labor costs are lower, and workers are highly trained. The city of Bengaluru (Bangalore) alone has more than 200 computer companies.

India and the World

Gandhi's ideas of civil disobedience had a lasting influence. Dr. Martin Luther King, Jr., in the United States and Nelson Mandela in South Africa, for example, used nonviolent protest to win equal rights. Dr. King said, "The choice is clearly between nonviolence and nonexistence."

QUICK CHECK

Compare and Contrast **How are Gandhi and Dr. King alike? How are they different?**

Check Understanding

1. **VOCABULARY** Write a newspaper article about modern India, using these terms:

   civil disobedience **Green Revolution**

2. **READING SKILL** Make Judgments Why do you think people say that Gandhi was an important leader?

Action	→	Judgment
	→	
	→	
	→	

3. **Essential Question** **Write About It** What caused conflict between the British and the people of India?

SEARCHING FOR PEACE

Presidents Sadat of Egypt (right), Carter of the United States (center), and Prime Minister Begin of Israel in 1978

Essential Question

Where did conflicts break out in Southwest Asia?

A Modern Israel has had conflicts with its neighbors since 1948.

B Iran, Afghanistan, and Iraq have experienced conflict.

THE BIRTH OF MODERN ISRAEL

"After four wars during 30 years, despite intensive human efforts, the Middle East...does not enjoy the blessings of peace." These are the first words of one treaty in troubled Southwest Asia.

In A.D. 70, the Romans drove the Jews out of ancient Israel. Ever since, Jews have lived throughout the world, but they always maintained their religion, customs, and traditions. Jews often endured discrimination. Discrimination against Jews is called **anti-Semitism**.

Looking for a Homeland

In the late 1800s, some Jews wanted to reestablish the nation of Israel as a homeland for Jews, and some began moving to the lands that had been ancient Israel. This region of Southwest Asia was called Palestine. (Arab residents of the area are still called Palestinians.) After World War II, many Holocaust survivors felt that Jews deserved to live in this area.

In 1948, the United Nations divided Palestine into Jewish and Arab areas. On May 14, Jews in Palestine declared the independence of their nation, Israel. Armies from five Arab neighbors attacked the new nation and were defeated.

Peace and Unrest

The United States has tried to bring peace to the region. In 1977, the leaders of Egypt and Israel met with President Jimmy Carter at Camp David, the presidential estate in Maryland. The leaders signed the Camp David Accords in 1978. An accord is an agreement. The Camp David Accords ended fighting between Egypt and Israel.

In a 1967 war, Israel captured the West Bank of the Jordan River. Palestinians have tried to win this land back with diplomacy and sometimes through violence. Palestinians created the Palestinian Liberation Organization or PLO. Its leader was Yasir Arafat. After his death in 2004, Palestinians elected Mahmoud Abbas as their new leader. The conflict between Palestinians and Israelis is a major cause of unrest in the region today.

QUICK CHECK

Make Judgments Why are the Camp David Accords important?

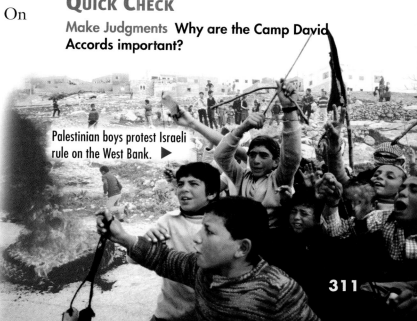

Palestinian boys protest Israeli rule on the West Bank. ▶

TROUBLED TIMES

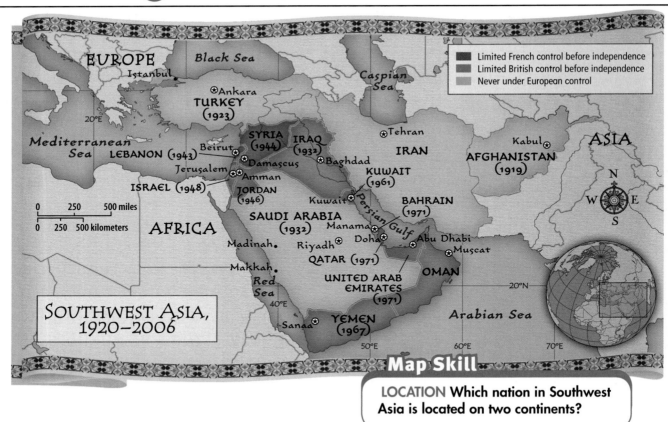

SOUTHWEST ASIA, 1920–2006

Limited French control before independence
Limited British control before independence
Never under European control

Map Skill

LOCATION Which nation in Southwest Asia is located on two continents?

Since World War II, there have been many conflicts and problems in Southwest Asia.

Iran

In 1979, the shah, or king, of Iran was driven from power. Muslim religious leaders took power and continue to rule the country. Iran's laws come from **sharia**, or laws followed by Muslims. Sharia laws control business, government, family life, and even clothing.

After 2000, Iran began to develop nuclear weapons. Many nations are concerned about Iran's development of these weapons.

Afghanistan

In 1978, troops from the Soviet Union invaded Afghanistan. About ten years later, Soviet troops left, but civil war followed. In 1996, a group called the Taliban seized power.

Taliban leaders were hostile to the United States and helped the planners of a terrorist attack in the United States. On September 11, 2001, four American passenger planes were hijacked. Two of the planes crashed into the World Trade Center in New York City. In Washington, D. C., another hijacked plane crashed into the Pentagon. Passengers attacked the hijackers of the fourth plane, and it crashed in a field in Pennsylvania. Nearly 3,000 people died in these attacks.

Osama bin Laden was the **terrorist** leader responsible for the September 11 attacks. A terrorist is someone who uses fear and violence to achieve political goals. Bin Laden was living in Afghanistan at the time of the attacks. In 2001, the United States and its allies invaded Afghanistan and defeated the Taliban leaders.

Under a new government, Mohammad Karzai became president of Afghanistan. Taliban fighters continued their attacks. The country lies in ruins after many years of war.

The Iraqi Wars

Iraq was ruled by a dictator, Saddam Hussein. In 1990, the Iraqi army invaded Kuwait, another nation in Southwest Asia. United Nations troops led by the United States drove the Iraqis out of Kuwait.

A second Iraq war began in 2003. American troops quickly captured Baghdad, Iraq's capital. Saddam Hussein lost power and was executed in 2006. The war lasted longer than expected, and U.S. troops are still there today. Violence between religious groups in Iraq makes the conflict more difficult.

QUICK CHECK

Sequence Events Make a time line of events in Southwest Asia, starting in 1978.

Check Understanding

1. **VOCABULARY** Write a summary of this lesson, using these words.

   anti-Semitism   terrorist

   Sharia

2. **READING SKILL Make Judgments** Use the chart to explain why you think the United States wants to end conflicts in Southwest Asia.

Action	→	Judgment
	→	
	→	
	→	

3. **Write About It** Discuss the main conflicts in Southwest Asia.

Essential Question

American soldiers on patrol in an Iraqi city in 2005

313

INDEPENDENCE IN AFRICA

Lesson 7

VOCABULARY

apartheid p. 315

sanctions p. 315

refugee p. 316

READING SKILL

Make Judgments

Complete the chart. Write ideas from the lesson. You will use your chart to make judgments about what you have read.

Action	→	Judgment
	→	
	→	
	→	

STANDARDS FOCUS

SOCIAL STUDIES Civic Ideals and Practices

GEOGRAPHY Place and Regions

Citizens celebrating independence day in Togo

Essential Question

How have modern Africans dealt with conflicts and challenges?

A After 1945, many African nations demanded freedom from colonial rule.

B African nations have cooperated to try to end civil wars and poverty.

C African nations have worked with world agencies to meet their challenges.

A NEW NATIONS IN AFRICA

Kwame Nkrumah lived in a British colony called Gold Coast. Like Gandhi in India, he organized boycotts and strikes against British rule. In 1957, the Gold Coast became the independent nation of Ghana.

Liberia and Ethiopia were the only African nations that were not European colonies in 1950. Inspired by the nation of Ghana, other African nations demanded independence. In 1960, the Belgian colony of Congo ended colonial rule. In the same year, Cote d'Ivoire (the Ivory Coast) ended French rule. Jomo Kenyatta freed Kenya from British rule in 1963. By 1970, few European colonies remained in Africa.

South African Freedom

South Africa proved to be a special case. In the late 1940s, a government of white settlers set up **apartheid**, a system that legally separated the races. Under apartheid, South Africans were grouped as either black, white, Asian, or colored (mixed ancestry). Blacks could not vote or hold certain jobs. The best neighborhoods, schools, and hospitals were reserved for whites. Non whites had to carry a pass to travel in white areas.

Nelson Mandela, a South African leader, fought apartheid. He spent 27 years in jail and became a hero to many South Africans. Other nations opposed apartheid by establishing **sanctions**, economic and cultural penalties, against the South African government. In 1990, Mandela was released from prison. In 1993, a new constitution gave all South Africans the right to vote. The next year, South Africans elected Nelson Mandela president. Apartheid had ended, but South Africa still faced many challenges.

QUICK CHECK

Make Judgments Why do you think South Africans elected Nelson Mandela president?

A South African celebrates the election of Nelson Mandela as president. ▶

315

B AFRICAN TROUBLES

▲ A doctor in Niger gives a child a checkup.

In 1963, African leaders voted to create the Organization of African Unity (OAU) to support African independence and cooperation. Except for Morocco, every country in Africa belongs to the OAU. The group now is known as African Union (AU).

War and Poverty

Civil wars have torn apart several African countries. One of Africa's first civil wars broke out in Nigeria in 1967. Nearly a million people died before the fighting ended in 1970. Angola had the longest civil war, lasting nearly 27 years. In addition to deaths from the fighting, wars cause deaths from hunger and illness. Wars also create **refugees**. These are people who leave their homes to escape death or suffering. Numerous large refugee camps still exist in Africa today.

One of the worst civil wars occurred in Rwanda in 1994. The majority Hutu ethnic group in Rwanda seized power in 1994. Some leaders then led a violent attack on the Tutsi minority group. More than 800,000 people were killed.

African nations have faced other challenges. The populations of many African nations have grown because Africans now live longer. Traditional farms have been abandoned, and people have moved to cities looking for work.

However, African economies do not provide enough jobs. Education is also a problem. Thousands of people live in poverty because they are unable to read or write.

Many African nations have great wealth in minerals or natural resources. When they are extracted, however, the money is not always fairly shared. As a result, the economies of many African nations are weak or unstable.

QUICK CHECK

Make Judgments **What do you think is the most serious challenge Africans face?**

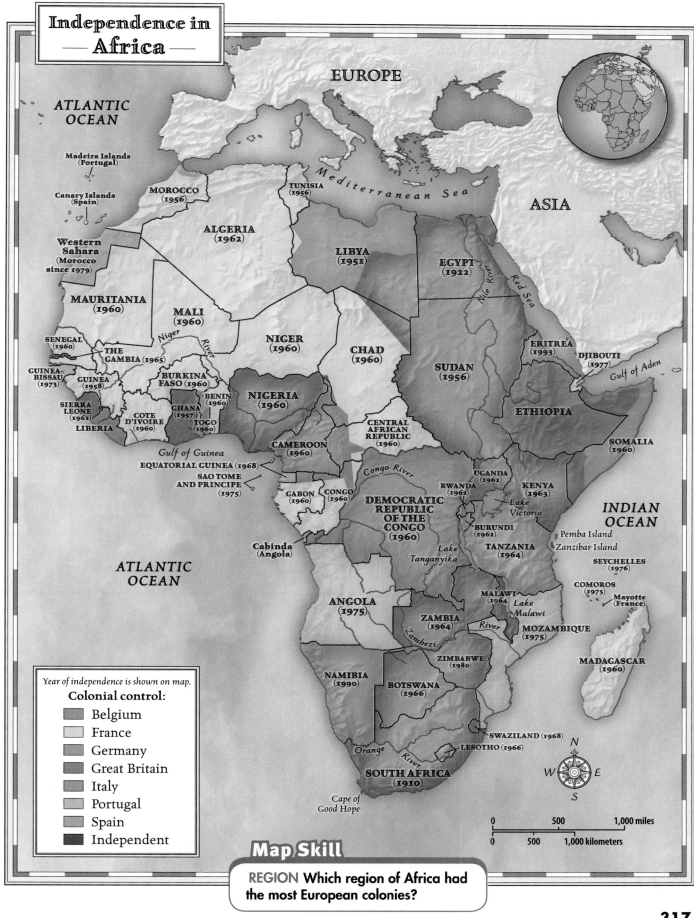

Independence in Africa

EUROPE

ATLANTIC OCEAN

ASIA

Madeira Islands (Portugal)

Canary Islands (Spain)

Mediterranean Sea

MOROCCO (1956)

TUNISIA (1956)

ALGERIA (1962)

LIBYA (1951)

EGYPT (1922)

Nile River

Red Sea

Western Sahara (Morocco since 1979)

MAURITANIA (1960)

MALI (1960)

NIGER (1960)

CHAD (1960)

SUDAN (1956)

ERITREA (1993)

DJIBOUTI (1977)

Gulf of Aden

Niger River

SENEGAL (1960)

THE GAMBIA (1965)

GUINEA-BISSAU (1973)

GUINEA (1958)

BURKINA FASO (1960)

BENIN (1960)

NIGERIA (1960)

SIERRA LEONE (1961)

LIBERIA

COTE D'IVOIRE (1960)

GHANA (1957)

TOGO (1960)

CENTRAL AFRICAN REPUBLIC (1960)

ETHIOPIA

SOMALIA (1960)

Gulf of Guinea

CAMEROON (1960)

EQUATORIAL GUINEA (1968)

SAO TOME AND PRINCIPE (1975)

GABON (1960)

CONGO (1960)

Congo River

DEMOCRATIC REPUBLIC OF THE CONGO (1960)

UGANDA (1962)

RWANDA (1962)

Lake Victoria

KENYA (1963)

INDIAN OCEAN

BURUNDI (1962)

TANZANIA (1964)

Pemba Island

Zanzibar Island

Cabinda (Angola)

Lake Tanganyika

ATLANTIC OCEAN

SEYCHELLES (1976)

COMOROS (1975)

Mayotte (France)

ANGOLA (1975)

MALAWI (1964)

Lake Malawi

MOZAMBIQUE (1975)

ZAMBIA (1964)

Zambezi River

MADAGASCAR (1960)

ZIMBABWE (1980)

NAMIBIA (1990)

BOTSWANA (1966)

SWAZILAND (1968)

Orange River

LESOTHO (1966)

SOUTH AFRICA (1910)

Cape of Good Hope

N
W E
S

Year of independence is shown on map.

Colonial control:

- Belgium
- France
- Germany
- Great Britain
- Italy
- Portugal
- Spain
- Independent

0   500   1,000 miles
0   500   1,000 kilometers

Map Skill

REGION **Which region of Africa had the most European colonies?**

Today there are 53 nations in Africa. Most of them still have the borders first used by European colonizers. While many of these nations are republics and have presidents, most are not really democratic. The governments are not always representative, and ethnic groups struggle for power. Many African nations have fallen under military rule, and a few have had brutal dictators.

Recent Trends

Outside agencies have worked to help Africans meet the challenges of the 21ST century. African governments can borrow money from the World Bank. For instance, the government of Kenya borrowed $7 million from the World Bank to expand its electricity service. Other African nations have used loans from the World Bank to improve transportation and health projects.

Africans want to find solutions to their own challenges, too. The AU is one way of bringing Africans together. In the Primary Sources box on this page, Kwame Nkrumah, the first president of Ghana, explains the purpose of African unity.

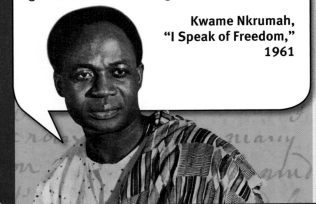

Primary Sources

"It is clear that we must find an African solution to our problems, and that this can only be found in African unity. Divided we are weak; united, Africa could become one of the greatest forces for good in the world."

**Kwame Nkrumah,
"I Speak of Freedom,"
1961**

Write About It What did Kwame Nkrumah want Africans to do?

OAU leaders at a meeting in Togo in 2000 ▼

African nations have been working to improve their continent. The AU is currently working in Sudan, where an ongoing civil war has led to hundreds of thousands of deaths. AU peacekeepers are trying to police the area of Darfur, in western Sudan.

Some African governments are weak, but they are making progress. Liberia elected the continent's first woman leader. Ellen Johnson-Sirleaf supports many of Nelson Mandela's ideas of freedom and equality. There is hope for the future because Africa is a continent with rich natural resources.

Building the Future

The two biggest challenges for Africa are food and health. Years of warfare and bad planning have left many Africans without enough food. In addition, many roads are so bad that farmers cannot bring their crops to markets. As a result, many Africans suffer from malnutrition, the lack of food or a form of starvation where the food does not contain enough vitamins and minerals. African governments and world scientists are working to improve crops and to find ways to bring these crops to market.

In addition, many African nations are too poor to provide basic health care for their people. Common diseases, such as measles, still kill many Africans each year. Other diseases, such as polio, leave many people crippled.

The worst disease in Africa today is Acquired Immune Deficiency Syndrome (AIDS). AIDS is a disease that destroys the body's ability to protect itself from infections or disease. African governments are working with outside governments and with private foundations to fight the AIDS epidemic.

Ellen Johnson-Sirleaf, Africa's first female president ▶

Education

Another challenge for Africa's future is education. Civil wars have interrupted the school years of many of Africa's children. Also, many Africans live far from cities. Their villages do not have schools or teachers. African governments are working with outside governments and other organizations to build schools and train teachers to educate future Africans.

QUICK CHECK

Make Judgments **Why might Africans want to find solutions to their own problems?**

Check Understanding

1. **VOCABULARY** Write an Internet article using these vocabulary words.

   apartheid   sanctions   refugee

2. **READING SKILL** Make Judgments Use the chart to make a judgment about Africa today. Be sure to support your opinion with lesson facts.

Action	→	Judgment
→		
→		
→		

Essential Question 3. **Write About It** Describe how conflicts have affected life in modern Africa.

319

Southeast Asia and the Pacific

Lesson 8

VOCABULARY

archipelago p. 321

coup p. 321

guerrilla p. 322

martial law p. 323

READING SKILL

Make Judgments

Complete the chart with ideas from the lesson. You will use the chart to make a judgment about what you have read.

Action	→	Judgment
	→	
	→	
	→	

STANDARDS FOCUS

SOCIAL STUDIES Global Connections

GEOGRAPHY Environment and Society

Protestors in Indonesia in 2005

Essential Question — What conflicts occurred in Southeast Asia in modern times?

A Indonesia became an independent nation after ending Dutch rule.

B Some new nations had civil wars or martial law.

C Pacific nations are becoming part of the global economy.

320

A INDONESIA'S INDEPENDENCE

After World War II, European colonies in Southeast Asia struggled to become independent. These new nations faced many challenges.

Find Indonesia on the map on page 324. Indonesia is the world's largest **archipelago**, or large group of islands. Indonesia includes more than 18,000 islands scattered along the Equator between the Indian and Pacific oceans. You have read how the archipelago became a Dutch colony called the Dutch East Indies. Indonesians resisted Dutch rule, and rebellions broke out many times. They were put down by the Dutch, but only with much difficulty.

During World War II, the islands were overrun by the armies of Japan. Resistance to the Japanese invaders was led by a man named Sukarno. When the war ended in 1945, Sukarno declared independence. The Dutch fought to keep their colony, but the islands became the independent nation of Indonesia in 1949.

Indonesia Today

In 1967, Sukarno was forced out of office after a **coup**. A coup is a sudden overthrow of a government by force. The new leader, a military dictator called Suharto, was responsible for killing as many as 750,000 people for political reasons. A decline in the world economy caused hardships for Indonesians in the late 1990s. People rioted over rising prices, foreign debts, and failed businesses. Suharto was forced to resign in 1998. Three years later, Sukarno's daughter, Megawati Sukarnoputri, became president.

In 2004, a tsunami, or tidal wave, wrecked many of Indonesia's islands. Thousands of people were killed. Terrorists caused further suffering when they bombed a vacation spot on the Indonesian island of Bali. Indonesia's government and people are working to overcome the challenges their nation faces.

QUICK CHECK

Making Judgments Why might a nation of 18,000 islands be especially difficult to rule?

Megawati Sukarnoputri shows her thumb to prove she had voted in Indonesian elections in 2004. ▼

THE END OF COLONIAL RULE

The French colonized Vietnam, Cambodia, and Laos in the 1800s. They called the region Indochina because it had long been influenced by India and by China.

Japanese armies conquered Indochina during World War II. When Japan was defeated in 1945, however, the French were unable to regain control of their colonies. Vietnam and Laos declared independence in 1949. Cambodia gained its freedom in 1953, but independence did not bring peace for that nation. **Guerrillas**, small groups who lead surprise attacks,

began civil wars. The wars ended and Cambodia became a democracy in the 1990s.

Vietnam

In 1954, communist guerrillas defeated the French forces that had controlled Vietnam. The country was divided into a communist north and a democratic south. Vietnam became part of the Cold War when the United States decided to support South Vietnam against the communist north. The United States provided money, weapons, and soldiers. By 1968, about half a million U.S. troops were fighting in Vietnam.

Some Americans began to oppose the war and held protests and demonstrations. The last American soldiers left in 1973 without a clear victory. Two years later,

City Hall in Ho Chi Minh City, Vietnam

▲ American soldiers on patrol during the Vietnam War in 1968

communists captured South Vietnam. More than 58,000 Americans had died in the war. Nearly two million Vietnamese died as well. More than a million Vietnamese fled the communist conquerors in small open boats.

For many years, the United States had little contact with Vietnam. Then, in the 1990s, the United States signed a treaty of friendship with Vietnam. In 1995, the two countries once again began to trade.

The Philippines

Spain ruled the Philippines for more than 350 years. In 1898, the United States captured the islands during the Spanish-American War. In 1946, the Philippines became an independent nation.

Ferdinand Marcos was elected president of the Philippines in 1965. His rule became increasingly corrupt. In 1972, Marcos declared that he would rule by **martial law**. Martial law is control of a country by the military. Benigno Aquino, a democratic leader, was murdered by Marcos supporters in 1983.

The Filipino people demanded an end to Marcos's rule in 1986. They elected Corazon Aquino, the widow of the slain leader, to succeed Marcos. Democracy gradually returned to the Philippines.

Corazon Aquino was followed by President Gloria Arroyo. She joins Michelle Bachelet of Chile as one of a growing number of female national leaders. Aquino, Arroyo, and Bachelet have worked to bring together former enemies within their countries.

Myanmar

The British colony of Burma became independent in 1948. Aung San, the man who led the fight for independence, was assassinated just before his nation gained its freedom. In 1962, Ne Win, a general, seized power. His government changed the country's name to Myanmar, the ancient name of the country.

The military rulers of Burma have been harsh and have ruined Burma's economy. In the People box, you will read about Aung San's daughter, who has led the resistance to the military rule. She has become a symbol of democracy in the fight for real elections.

QUICK CHECK

Sequence of Events **Make a time line of events in Southeast Asia since World War II.**

PEOPLE

Aung San's daughter, **Aung San Suu Kyi**, led the fight to restore democracy. In 1990, Aung San Suu Kyi was elected president of Myanmar. The military rulers arrested her, so she could not take power. In 1991, she won a Nobel Prize for Peace.

Aung San Suu Kyi

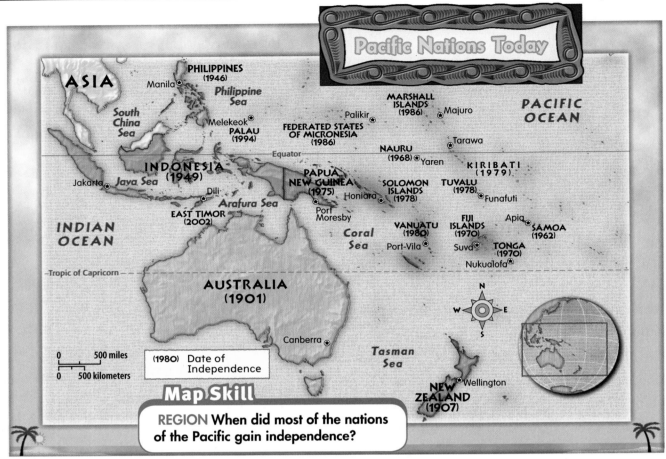

Pacific Nations Today

ASIA

PHILIPPINES
(1946)
Manila

Philippine
Sea

South
China
Sea

Melekeok
PALAU
(1994)

FEDERATED STATES
OF MICRONESIA
(1986)

MARSHALL
ISLANDS
(1986)
Majuro

Palikir

PACIFIC
OCEAN

Equator

NAURU
(1968)
Yaren

Tarawa

KIRIBATI
(1979)

INDONESIA
(1949)

Jakarta
Java Sea

Dili

Arafura Sea

EAST TIMOR
(2002)

PAPUA
NEW GUINEA
(1975)

Port
Moresby

SOLOMON
ISLANDS
(1978)
Honiara

TUVALU
(1978)
Funafuti

INDIAN
OCEAN

VANUATU
(1980)

Port-Vila

Coral
Sea

FIJI
ISLANDS
(1970)

Suva

Apia
SAMOA
(1962)

TONGA
(1970)

Nukualofa

Tropic of Capricorn

AUSTRALIA
(1901)

N
W E
S

Canberra

Tasman
Sea

0   500 miles
0   500 kilometers

(1980) Date of
Independence

Map Skill

NEW
ZEALAND
(1907)

Wellington

REGION When did most of the nations
of the Pacific gain independence?

A rim is the edge of a bowl or basket. The "Pacific Rim" describes nations around the edge of the Pacific Ocean. Many of these Pacific nations are affecting the economy of the world.

Little Tigers

The word "tiger" makes people think of fierce power. So it is no surprise that four small, successful economies in Asia have been called "Little Tigers." They are South Korea, Taiwan, Hong Kong (part of China since 1997), and Singapore. They have become major manufacturing and banking centers.

In the mid-1990s, these countries had an economic boom. There was an economic downturn in the late 1990s, but they are recovering and are still centers of world trade.

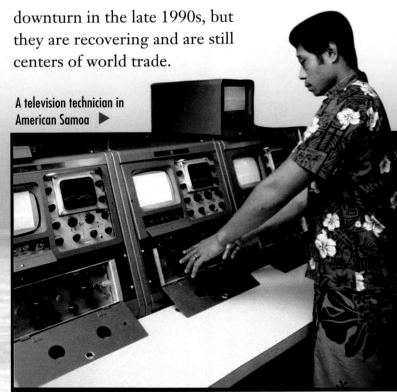

A television technician in American Samoa ▶

Australia and New Zealand

Australia and New Zealand have similar histories. Both were British colonies in the 1800s. People were already living in both countries for centuries when the British arrived. Today these native cultures form a part of the culture of each nation.

English colonists developed large sheep ranches in New Zealand and Australia. These nations also exported wool and leather products to the rest of the world.

In the early 1900s, Australia and New Zealand became self-governing nations within the British Empire. Great Britain's Queen Elizabeth II, however, is still the queen of Australia and of New Zealand.

▲ A farmer and his dog herd sheep in New Zealand.

Island Nations

After World War II, the United Nations put most Pacific islands under the care of larger nations, such as the United States or Great Britain. People on the islands were allowed to vote, and almost all of these islands have now become independent nations. Because they are dotted across the Pacific Ocean, these island nations are sometimes called Oceania.

All of these nations have become part of the global economy. Today some Pacific islands are banking centers. Others have become bases for international Internet sites. Still others have become centers of manufacturing.

QUICK CHECK

Make Inferences Why might banking or the Internet be good industries for a Pacific island nation?

Check Understanding

1. **VOCABULARY** Write a brief guide to Southeast Asia using these words.

   archipelago   guerrilla

   coup   martial law

2. **READING SKILL** Make Judgments Suppose you were a leader of one of the newly independent nations in this lesson. Use your completed chart to explain what you want for your new country.

Action	→	Judgment
	→	
	→	
	→	

3. **Write About It** Write a newspaper story telling how one of the countries in this lesson became independent. Remember your first paragraph should state *who, what, where, when,* and *why.*

   Essential Question

Global Challenges

Lesson 9

VOCABULARY

global economy p. 327

globalization p. 327

READING SKILL

Make Judgments
Complete the chart with ideas from this lesson. You will use your chart to write about the lesson.

Action	→	Judgment
	→	
	→	
	→	

STANDARDS FOCUS

SOCIAL STUDIES Production, Distribution, and Consumption

GEOGRAPHY Environment and Society

Leaders of industrial nations meet with African leaders in Canada in 2002.

Essential Question

What are some of the challenges facing the nations of the world today?

A Most nations must adjust their economies to participate in the global economy.

B The world's people are working to end poverty and threats to the environment.

C Today people are working together to find causes and cures for diseases.

D People around the world work together to solve global problems.

326

A A NEW ECONOMY

Modern nations are interdependent. They rely on one another to meet their needs. These needs include raw materials, the production of goods, and markets for selling the goods.

Just like people, governments cooperate to get things done. Working together helps nations get the materials and products they need. Cooperation among nations has created a worldwide economic system, called the **global economy**.

A Worldwide System

The global economy is a characteristic of **globalization**, or worldwide interdependence. Globalization also includes the spread of economies, technology, culture, and politics among countries. Modern communication and transportation make it possible to work in one country and have customers in another. New ideas and cultures spread as products move along trade routes.

The World Trade Organization (WTO) enforces the rules of a global economy. WTO supporters say that it creates cheaper products.

People who oppose the WTO believe it benefits large companies and more powerful countries. Critics claim that it costs jobs and replaces traditional cultures with imported products and customs.

An Internet World

The Internet is a worldwide system of connected computer networks. It helps make globalization possible. By 1996, over one billion people were using the Internet. The number of worldwide users continues to increase.

Businesses can buy and sell goods using the internet. People also are using the internet to purchase and sell goods. Most important, it makes communication much easier than before.

QUICK CHECK

Making Judgments **Why do you think people disagree about globalization?**

A container ship unloads cargo at Los Angeles, California. ▶

It is important to protect the environment. Gases from factories and automobiles and garbage in rivers and soil pollute our air and water. Also, the world's population has been growing quickly. This growth has strained natural resources, especially in poorer parts of the world. People have used up water, farmland, and forests. A region that once supported villages can become a desert.

Global Warming

Global warming is an increase in the average temperature on Earth. It is caused by an increase in gases, especially carbon dioxide, in the atmosphere surrounding Earth. Much of this carbon dioxide comes from automobile exhaust or factory smoke. The United States has only about five percent of the world's population, but it produces about 22 percent of the world's carbon dioxide.

Deforestation increases the effects of global warming. Deforestation occurs when people cut down forests. Forests remove carbon dioxide from the air. As trees are cut down, less carbon dioxide is absorbed, and temperatures rise.

Global warming could change weather around the world. Storms could become more common, and there might be more hurricanes and tornadoes. Global warming is causing ice at the North and South Poles to melt. Arctic animals and plants are in danger, and melting ice is already raising sea levels. Cities along the seacoast may be flooded, and people may have to move inland. Some island nations could disappear entirely.

Natural Disasters

Sometimes natural forces cause great damage. These include earthquakes, volcanoes, hurricanes, and floods. In 2004, an earthquake in the Indian Ocean caused a large wave known as a tsunami. About 225,000 people in Southeast Asia died when the tsunami hit land, making it one of the worst natural disasters in history.

The rainforest is losing 200,000 acres every day. ▶

▲ The tsunami of 2005 left destruction in its path.

During 2005, 13 hurricanes hit the United States. Seven of them were major storms. The worst of these storms was Hurricane Katrina. It caused more than $30 billion in damages to Louisiana, Mississippi, and the Gulf Coast.

Scientists continue to look for ways to protect us and to use Earth's resources wisely. There are warning systems for some natural disasters, for example. An early tsunami warning system might have saved thousands of lives in Southeast Asia. Had equipment like this been in use it might have saved thousands of lives in 2004.

QUICK CHECK

Cause and Effect What are some causes of global warming?

DataGraphic
Carbon Dioxide and You

The six countries in this DataGraphic are members of the Group of 8, the countries with the highest Gross Domestic Product (GDP). Study the graphs and answer the questions.

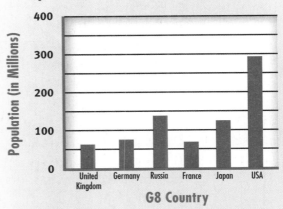

Population of Some G8 Nations in 2000

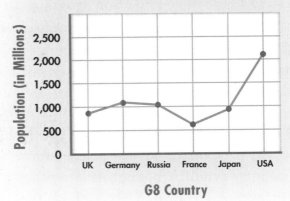

CO_2 Emissions Per Capita in G8 Countries (in tons)

Think About CO_2

1. Which country has the highest per capita (per person) carbon dioxide emissions?

2. Why might some of the other countries have lower per capita numbers?

329

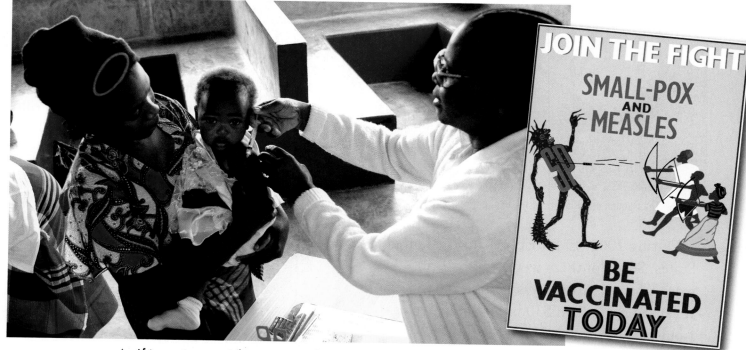

▲ African nations are working to wipe out diseases. This health care worker vaccinates a child against measles. The poster (right) reminds citizens to be vaccinated.

Disease has been a challenge since history began. Today most industrialized countries have the technology to prevent and treat many illnesses. There are vaccination programs to prevent common diseases, such as measles or mumps. Scientists continue to look for new medicines and treatments for diseases, such as cancer and heart disease.

The End of Smallpox

Because of modern air travel, diseases in one country can be brought easily to other countries. Some countries do not have the doctors or technology they need to prevent these diseases. These countries need help from richer nations and from the United Nations. They also need trained health care workers and medicines to vaccinate their people and to plan prevention programs.

The end of smallpox is one public health success story. For centuries smallpox had killed millions of people. You have read how Edward Jenner discovered a vaccination for smallpox in the 1790s. The World Health Organization (WHO) is a part of the United Nations. In 1967, the WHO made plans to end smallpox forever. There is a vaccine for smallpox, but no cure once the disease infects a person.

The WHO made plans to vaccinate everyone on Earth. The organization also isolated villages with smallpox to prevent the spread of the disease. Local people were trained to watch for the disease and to report its outbreak immediately.

In 1977, the last case of smallpox was reported in Somalia. Since that year, no new cases have occurred. The world seems to be free of this dreaded, killer disease.

Other diseases continue to cause suffering around the world. Of these, the most serious threat to health is AIDS, which you have read about. It has swept across the world, killing hundreds of thousands. There is no vaccination for AIDS, and there is no cure. The WHO and other groups are studying programs and policies that would help to halt the spread of this terrible killer.

Helping New Nations

Since World War II, the United States and other countries have tried to help newly independent nations. The Peace Corps, for example, is an American organization that sends teachers, doctors, and advisers to struggling areas. Other international organizations work to provide better crops and clean water for villages.

Until the new nations have enough food and safe water, diseases will continue to be a serious challenge.

QUICK CHECK

Cause and Effect **Why do some nations have more outbreaks of diseases than others?**

Citizenship
Working for the Common Good

For centuries, people had no way to avoid epidemics of smallpox. The disease was conquered when people worked together to keep it from spreading. Most public health issues require everyone to work together. Nurses and doctors can provide medicines and care, but ordinary people—neighbors, friends, family— must also help by identifying those who are ill and by getting them the medical care they need. Many countries hold practice "emergencies" so that everyone knows what to do when a disease breaks out. Community organizers and ordinary people practice helping doctors and nurses bring help to those who need it.

Write About It Make a poster showing what villagers can do to help medical workers in their village.

Indian health care workers try to convince villagers to be vaccinated against polio. ▶

D THE WORLD OF TOMORROW

▲ The ruins of the Twin Towers burn in New York City the day after the September 11 attacks.

The future holds challenges and reasons for hope. We face serious problems, but hard work and cooperation can improve the world.

The Threat of War

Since 1945, atomic or nuclear weapons have made the threat of war even more frightening. The United States used two atom bombs during World War II. Since then, the Soviet Union, Britain, France, and China also developed nuclear weapons. The list of countries that have nuclear weapons is growing. More recently, India, Pakistan, Israel, and North Korea were also known to possess nuclear weapons.

As the number of nuclear weapons has grown, the threat of nuclear attack has increased. World leaders worry that these weapons could be used by terrorists.

Terrorism

The terrorist attacks in 2001 on the United States were led by the Afghanistan-based group called al Qaeda. After the attacks, the United States drove al Qaeda from Afghanistan. The group's international attacks, however, have continued. There have been bombings in Spain, Britain, and Indonesia.

Fighting terrorism is often more difficult than fighting a normal enemy. Terrorists are rarely associated with a nation. Finding a terrorist target to attack is difficult, as they live in secret and are often spread around the world. For a nation to fight terrorism, it must work very hard to collect good intelligence, or information, on terrorists.

A Hopeful Future

Government agencies, private organizations, and citizens are working to solve today's problems. International organizations, such as Doctors Without Borders, bring health and support services to isolated areas. Other agencies, run by governments, send money and supplies. Modern communications help these supplies to arrive quickly.

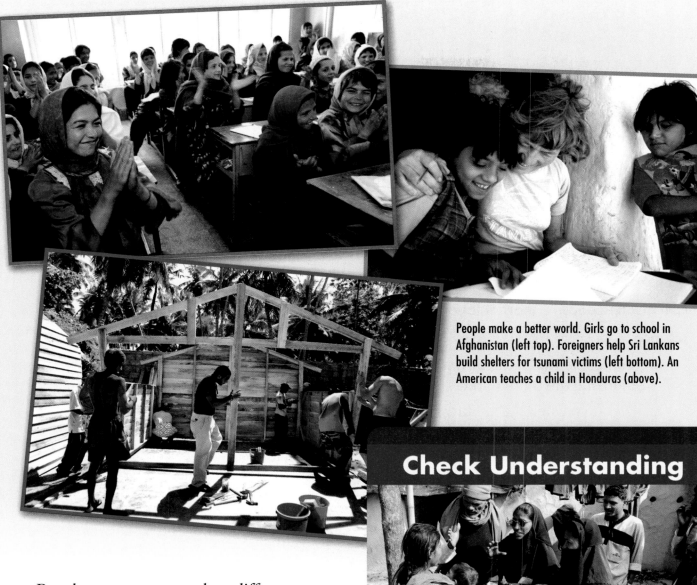

People make a better world. Girls go to school in Afghanistan (left top). Foreigners help Sri Lankans build shelters for tsunami victims (left bottom). An American teaches a child in Honduras (above).

People your age can make a difference, too. For example, a Canadian middle school student created an organization to fight child labor. Another young man collected money to dig wells in Africa. Individuals can make a difference and feel they are making a better future. You are an American and a citizen of the world. What would you like to do to make the world a better place?

QUICK CHECK

Make Judgments **Why do some groups use terror to win their goals?**

Check Understanding

1. **VOCABULARY** Write a paragraph about interdependence of the world's economy. Use these vocabulary terms.

   global economy   **globalization**

2. **READING SKILL** Make Judgments Use your chart to write a letter to a newspaper. Describe a challenge facing the United States. Be sure to include your ideas for solving the challenge.

Action	→	Judgment
	→	
	→	
	→	

3. **Write About It** Write about what you think might cause conflicts among people in the future.

 Essential Question

Vocabulary

Write the word from the list that matches the definition.

armistice   **space race**

civil disobedience **martial law**

refugee

1. a contest between the Soviet Union and the United States

2. a situation when the military rules a country

3. a person who flees from home to escape death or dangers

4. the refusal to obey an unjust law

5. an agreement to end fighting during a war

Comprehension and Critical Thinking

6. What was the Cold War?

7. **Reading Skill** Why do governments use sanctions?

8. How does a global economy make nations interdependent?

9. **Critical Thinking** How did the Cultural Revolution affect life in China?

10. **Critical Thinking** Why are Nazi Germany and the Soviet Union two examples of a totalitarian state?

Skill

Use a Cartogram

Write a complete sentence to answer each question.

11. Why is Brazil so large on this cartogram?

12. Why is Bolivia very small on this cartogram?

13. Which three countries have the largest economies?

South America: Gross Domestic Product

VENEZUELA GUYANA SURINAME

COLOMBIA

ECUADOR BRAZIL

PERU

BOLIVIA

PARAGUAY

CHILE URUGUAY

ARGENTINA

Each box represents 10 billion U.S. dollars

Test Preparation

Read the passage. Then answer the questions.

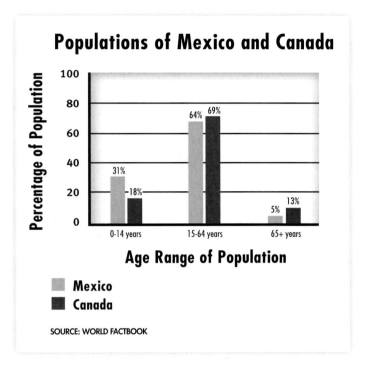

Populations of Mexico and Canada

Percentage of Population

31%
−18%
64% 69%
5% 13%

0-14 years   15-64 years   65+ years

Age Range of Population

■ **Mexico**
■ **Canada**

SOURCE: WORLD FACTBOOK

1. Which country has a larger percentage of people aged 0-14 years?

A. Mexico

B. They are the same

C. Canada

D. Not enough information

2. Which country has a larger percentage of elderly?

A. Mexico

B. They are the same

C. Canada

D. Not enough information

3. Why do you think the largest group in each country is 15-64?

A. It is the most common age.

B. This group covers the largest number of ages.

C. These people live longest.

D. These people have easier lives.

4. Which age range do you think contributes the most to its country's economy? Why?

5. Why do you think Mexico has a smaller percentage of people aged 65 and over?

What causes conflict among people?

Write About the Big Idea

Expository Essay

In Unit 6, you studied the many conflicts of the 20th Century. Review your foldable and decide which cause of conflict you will write about.

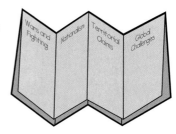

Begin with an introductory paragraph, which clearly states the cause of conflict you have chosen. Make a judgment about how this cause has created conflicts.

Write a paragraph using details from your foldable and from the unit to support your judgment.

Summarize your judgment in a final paragraph.

Have a Debate

Work with a partner to organize a debate. Look in a newspaper for a conflict either in your area or in the world. It might be a civil war, or it might be a local disagreement about how a public park will benefit the community.

1. Research the conflict and identify the two points of view.

2. Decide which side each person will represent in the debate.

3. Prepare your arguments and present a debate for your classmates.

4. Have your class make a judgment. They may vote to decide which side of the argument persuaded them it was correct.

Reference Section

The Reference Section has many parts, each with a different type of information. Use this section to look up people, places, and events as you study.

Draw Conclusions

When you read, look for the main ideas and details in each passage. Think about what you have read. You can use the information in a passage to draw a conclusion. Drawing a conclusion means deciding something, or having an opinion, about what you read.

Learn It

- Identify the main idea and important details in a passage.

- Ask yourself what you have learned from the passage.

- Use what you have read to draw a conclusion about the subject.

Read this passage and draw a conclusion about its main idea.

Leonardo da Vinci was a famous artist, but he actually painted very few works of art. His most famous paintings are the "Mona Lisa" and "The Last Supper." Few other major paintings by Leonardo exist today. Historians study Leonardo's notebooks to learn about projects he planned but did not complete. He filled nearly 13,000 pages in his notebooks with detailed drawings and scientific ideas. He produced plans for buildings, canals, bridges, flying machines, and even weapons, such as a tank. All of Leonardo's plans were based on careful study and observation of nature. His flying machines, for example, were based on detailed studies of birds in flight.

Details
Leonardo's notebooks include designs for inventions.

Conclusion
Leonardo was a creative and productive person.

Try It

Copy and complete the chart below using information from the paragraph on the previous page. First, list details from the text. Then write a conclusion based on the details you have listed.

Text Clues	Conclusion

What other conclusions could you draw about Leonardo?

Apply It

Read the paragraph below. Then, create a new chart. List details on your chart, and draw a conclusion about the subject of the paragraph.

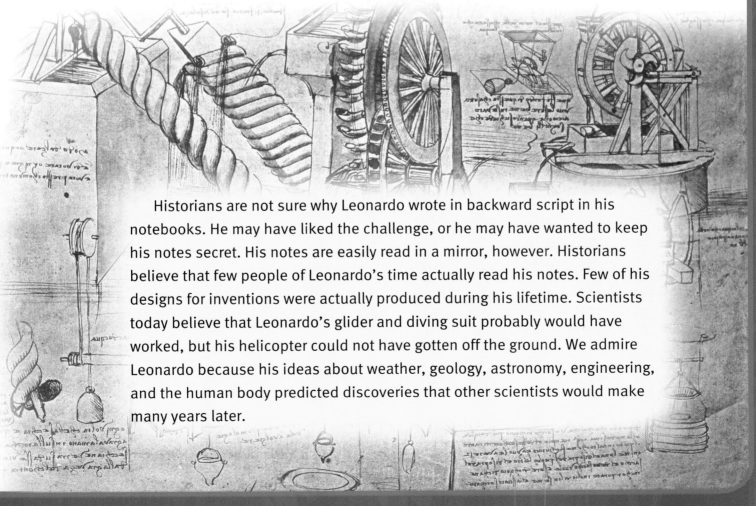

Historians are not sure why Leonardo wrote in backward script in his notebooks. He may have liked the challenge, or he may have wanted to keep his notes secret. His notes are easily read in a mirror, however. Historians believe that few people of Leonardo's time actually read his notes. Few of his designs for inventions were actually produced during his lifetime. Scientists today believe that Leonardo's glider and diving suit probably would have worked, but his helicopter could not have gotten off the ground. We admire Leonardo because his ideas about weather, geology, astronomy, engineering, and the human body predicted discoveries that other scientists would make many years later.

Make Inferences

Writers want their readers to think about what they have read and to make inferences, or guesses, about what happened. To do this, you think about what you know from other reading or from your own experience. You use both kinds of information to make an inference about something.

Learn It

As you read, identify the details and clues in the text.

- Combine the clues and details with what you already know.

- Make an inference by "reading between the lines."

- Read the passage below. Think about an inference you could make.

Clue Lafayette lost his father as a young boy.	The Marquis de Lafayette was born in France. His father died when he was two years old. When he heard of the American Revolution, he decided to sail to the young United States and fight for the Patriots. He had to buy his own ship and equipment, but he was made a general and worked on the staff of George Washington.
Detail Lafayette admired Washington and tried to imitate him.	Lafayette took Washington as a role model. Lafayette fought bravely and was wounded in battle. In 1779, he returned to France long enough to persuade the French government to support the American cause. Lafayette returned to the United States and fought at the Battle of Yorktown in 1781.

Try It

Copy the chart below. Then fill in the chart in order to make inferences about the Marquis de Lafayette.

Text Clues	What You Know	Generalization

What inferences can you make about Lafayette and Washington?

Apply It

Read the paragraphs below. Then use the information to make a new inference chart like the one above.

Lafayette wanted France to have a more democratic government. He supported the revolt against the king in 1789. However, the revolution turned more violent in 1791. The king was overthrown, and many people were executed. In 1792, a new French dictator began to arrest his enemies. Lafayette fled from France and did not return until 1800.

After Lafayette returned to France, he became a leader of resistance to French kings. In 1830, France had another revolution. Again the king was overthrown. Lafayette refused to become president of France. Instead, he supported a new king.

Make Judgments

People make judgments as they read. Making a judgment means forming an opinion about an event or the actions of a person in history. As you read, look for clues that either support or change your judgment.

Learn It

- Think about a historical person you are studying. What choices did he or she make?

- Make a judgment. Do you think the person's choices were good ones? Would you have made the same choices?

- Read the passage below. Make a judgment about the action taken by President Franklin Roosevelt as described in the passage.

Franklin Roosevelt became President of the United States in 1933. The American economy was in serious trouble. Stocks had lost much of their value. Many people had lost their jobs and, often, their homes. Worst of all, American banks were closing their doors. They had run out of money. Everyone was frightened. It was the new President's job to calm the nation. In his first speech as President, Roosevelt said, "We have nothing to fear but fear itself."

Action
Roosevelt realized that he had to calm the nation.

Judgment
What do you think of Roosevelt's decision to warn people about panic?

Try It

Copy the chart below. Complete it with actions and your judgments about the paragraph on the previous page.

Action	— ▶ Reasons for Action
	— ▶
	— ▶
	— ▶

What judgment would you make about Roosevelt's actions?

Apply It

Review the steps for making judgments. Complete a new chart for the paragraph below. Make a judgment about President Roosevelt's actions.

One of President Roosevelt's first acts was to close all the banks. He wanted people to think clearly about the future. He also wanted to be sure the banks could handle their customers' needs for cash. Then he went on the radio to tell Americans what would happen when the banks reopened. He closed his radio speech with these words. "Confidence and courage are the essentials of success in carrying out our plan. You people must have faith; you must not be stampeded by rumors or guesses. Let us unite in banishing fear."

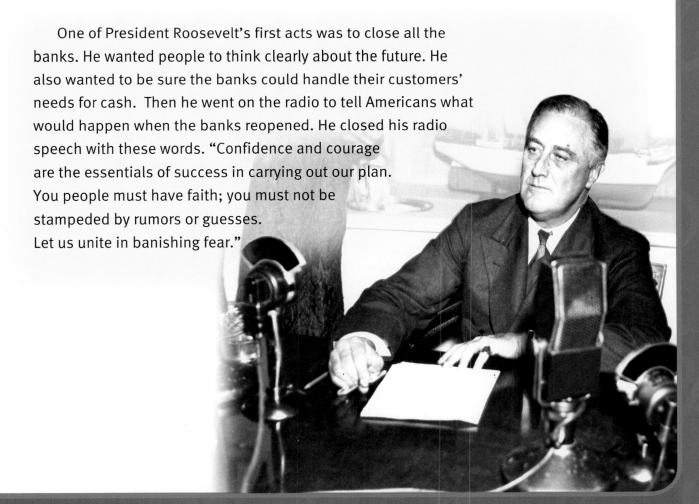

Geography Handbook

Geography and You

Geography is the study of many exciting things about our Earth and all of us who live here. Most people think of geography as learning about cities, states, and countries, but geography is more than that. Geography includes learning about bodies of water, such as oceans, lakes, and rivers. Geography also helps us learn about land, such as plains, mountains, and even volcanoes. Geography also helps people learn how to use land and water wisely.

People are part of geography, too. Geography includes the study of how people adapt to a new place in order to live there. How people move goods is also part of geography.

In fact, geography includes so many things that geographers have divided this information into six elements, or ideas, so you can better understand them.

Six Elements of Geography

The World in Spatial Terms: Where is a place located, and what land or water features does this place have?

Place and Region: What is special about a place, and what makes it different from other places?

Physical Systems: What has shaped the land and climate of a place, and how does this affect the plants, animals, and people there?

Human Systems: How do people, ideas, and goods move from place to place?

Environment and Society: How have people changed the land and water of a place, and how have the land and water affected the people of a place?

Uses of Geography: How does geography influence events of the past, present, and the future?

Five Themes of Geography

To understand how our world is connected, some geographers have broken down the study of geography into five different themes. The themes are **location, place, region, movement**, and **human interaction**. Understanding these themes will help you make sense of historical events.

1. Location

Location means an exact spot on the planet. A location can be defined in several ways. Usually it includes a street name and number. You write a location when you address a letter. Location can also be a set of numbers. These numbers relate to a geographical grid system called longitude and latitude. This imaginary grid helps geographers find locations on Earth that do not have street numbers.

Eiffel Tower in Paris, France

2. Place

Patagonia in Argentina

The description of a *place* is a combination of human and physical characteristics that make a place unique. To name a place, you would describe physical features, such as rivers, mountains, or valleys. You would also describe human characteristics of a place. This includes its population density, its major cities, or its language and religion.

3. Region

The Sahara in Algeria

A *region* is bigger than a place or a location. Regions cover large areas of land that share physical or human characteristics. For example, the nations of the Sahara have a hot, dry climate and populations that are centered near water. Other areas might be grouped because of cultural similarities. For example, many people of the Middle East share the religion of Islam.

4. Movement

Boats on the Grand Canal, China

Throughout history, there have been economic or political reasons for large numbers of people to *move* from one place to another. As people moved, they made changes, such as roads or canals. Cultures were often changed by encountering other cultures. Geographers look at why movements occur and how they affect cultures and environments.

5. Human Interaction

A wind farm in California

Geographers are interested in how the environment influences people. For example, people in cold areas need more fuel to generate heat in the winters. Geographers study how people adapt and change their environments. This *interaction* can determine how land is used for business, recreation, housing, and industry.

Dictionary of Geographic Terms

1 **BASIN** A bowl-shaped landform surrounded by higher land

2 **BAY** Part of an ocean or lake that extends deeply into the land

3 **CANAL** A channel built to carry water for irrigation or transportation

4 **CANYON** A deep, narrow valley with steep sides

5 **COAST** The land along an ocean

6 **DAM** A wall built across a river, creating a lake that stores water

7 **DELTA** Land made of soil left behind as a river drains into a larger body of water

8 **DESERT** A dry environment with few plants and animals

9 **FAULT** The border between two of the plates that make up Earth's crust

10 **GLACIER** A huge sheet of ice that moves slowly across the land

11 **GULF** Part of an ocean that extends into the land; larger than a bay

12 **HARBOR** A sheltered place along a coast where boats dock safely

13 **HILL** A rounded, raised landform; not as high as a mountain

14 **ISLAND** A body of land completely surrounded by water

15 **LAKE** A body of water completely surrounded by land

16 **MESA** A hill with a flat top; smaller than a plateau

17 **MOUNTAIN** A high landform with steep sides; higher than a hill

18 **MOUNTAIN PASS** A narrow gap through a mountain range

19 **MOUTH** The place where a river empties into a larger body of water

20 **OCEAN** A large body of salt water; oceans cover much of Earth's surface

21 **PENINSULA** A body of land nearly surrounded by water

22 **PLAIN** A large area of nearly flat land

23 **PLATEAU** A high, flat area that rises steeply above the surrounding land

24 **PORT** A place where ships load and unload their goods

25 **RESERVOIR** A natural or artificial lake used to store water

26 **RIVER** A stream of water that flows across the land and empties into another body of water

27 **SOURCE** The starting point of a river

28 **VALLEY** An area of low land between hills or mountains

29 **VOLCANO** An opening in Earth's surface through which hot rock and ash are forced out

30 **WATERFALL** A flow of water falling vertically

Reviewing Geography Skills

Read a Map

Most maps include standard features that help you understand the information on the map. One of the most important pieces of information you can get from a map is direction. The main directions are north, south, east, and west. These are called cardinal directions. Usually these directions on a map are indicated by a compass rose.

Map Title Maps in this book have titles. The map title names the area shown on the map. A map title can include additional identification, such as population, political boundaries, or a particular period in history.

Locator Map A locator map highlights the area of the main map on a small map of Earth. Locator maps help readers understand the region they are studying.

Inset Map An inset map is a small map set onto a larger map. It may show an area that is too small or too far away to be included on the main map. The inset map on this page calls out a more detailed map of the Himalaya, Earth's highest mountains.

Scale A map scale helps you to determine the relationship between real distances on Earth and the same distances represented on the map.

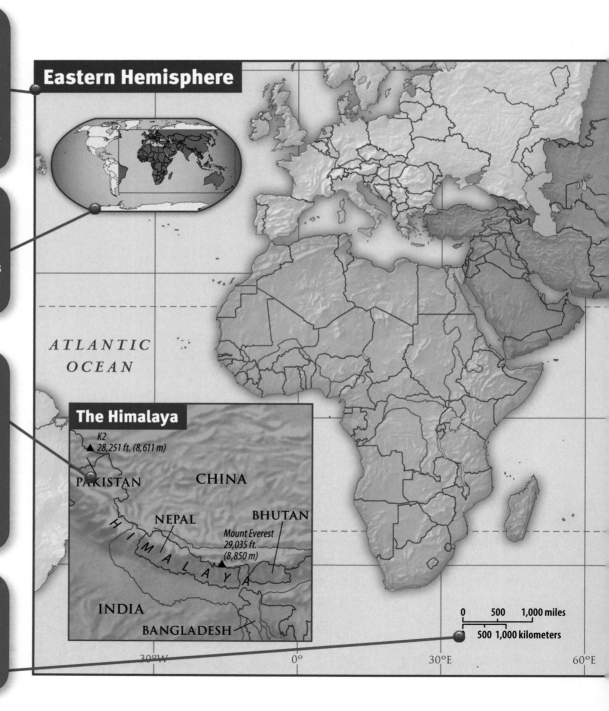

Eastern Hemisphere

ATLANTIC OCEAN

The Himalaya

K2
▲ 28,251 ft. (8,611 m)

PAKISTAN   CHINA

NEPAL   BHUTAN

Mount Everest
29,035 ft.
(8,850 m)

H I M A L A Y A

INDIA

BANGLADESH

0   500   1,000 miles

500 1,000 kilometers

30°W   0°   30°E   60°E

The areas between cardinal directions are called intermediate directions. These are northeast, northwest, southeast, and southwest. Intermediate directions let us describe a place in relation to another place. This is called the relative location of a place. If you look on the map on this page, you can see that the relative location of Australia and Oceania is southeast of Asia.

What kind of detailed information is given in the inset map?

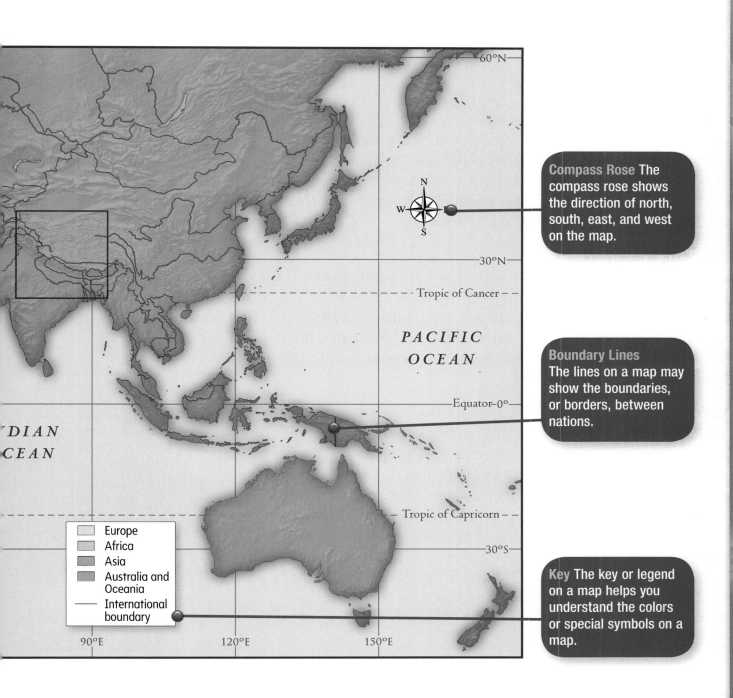

Compass Rose The compass rose shows the direction of north, south, east, and west on the map.

Boundary Lines The lines on a map may show the boundaries, or borders, between nations.

Key The key or legend on a map helps you understand the colors or special symbols on a map.

PACIFIC OCEAN

INDIAN OCEAN

60°N

30°N

Tropic of Cancer

Equator–0°

Tropic of Capricorn

30°S

90°E   120°E   150°E

Europe
Africa
Asia
Australia and Oceania
International boundary

Understand Earth

Hemispheres

Earth is often shown as a sphere, or a ball shape. A hemisphere is half of a sphere. Geographers have divided Earth into hemispheres. The area north of the equator is called the Northern Hemisphere. The area south of the equator is called the Southern Hemisphere.

The Prime Meridian runs north-south through Greenwich, England. Everything east of the Prime Meridian for 180 degrees is the Eastern Hemisphere. Everything west of the Prime Meridian for 180 degrees is the Western Hemisphere.

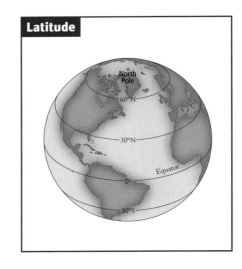

Latitude

Lines of latitude are called parallels because they are always at an equal distance from one another. Lines of latitude are numbered from 0 at the equator to 90 degrees north at the North Pole and 90 degrees south at the South Pole. Maps with latitude lines have N or S to indicate the Northern or Southern Hemisphere.

Longitude

Lines of longitude, or meridians, circle the Earth from pole to pole. These lines measure the distance from the Prime Meridian, 0 degrees longitude. Lines of longitude are not parallel. They grow closer together near the North and South Poles. At the equator, they are far apart. Maps have an E or a W next to the number to indicate the Eastern or Western Hemisphere.

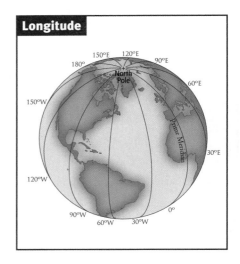

Absolute Location

You can locate any place on Earth using lines of latitude and longitude. Each line is identified by degrees (°). The spaces between the degree lines are measured in minutes ('). Each location has a unique number where one line of latitude intersects, or crosses, a line of longitude. This is absolute location. Each spot on Earth has an absolute location identified by a single set of degrees and minutes.

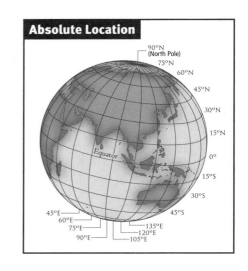

Think About It What is your absolute location? Use the map of the United States on page GH23 to find the lines of latitude and longitude that are closest to your home.

Special Purpose Maps

Some maps show specific information about a place or a period in history. These specific maps are called special purpose maps. One type of special purpose map may show how many people live in an area. Another may show the roads of a region. Still another might show the movement of an army during a historic battle.

Historical Maps

Some special purpose maps capture a period in time. These are called historical maps. They show information about past events, and the places where they occurred. Read the title of the map on this page and study the key to understand its information. The map shows information about a battle in 31 B.C. between Antony, a Roman general, and Octavian, the ruler of Rome. Octavian won the Battle of Actium. Antony's defeat helped Octavian to become the absolute ruler of the Mediterranean world.

Think About It Why might Octavian have placed his ships across the entrance to the Gulf of Ambracia?

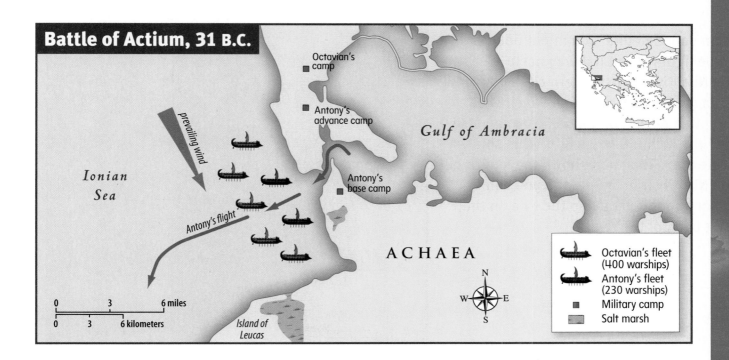

Battle of Actium, 31 B.C.

Maps at Different Scales

If you drew a map of the United States at its real size, your map would have to be over 3,000 miles wide. The Mississippi River on your map would be more than 2,000 miles long! A map this size would be too big to use!

So mapmakers draw maps to scale. A map scale uses some unit of measurement, such as an inch, to represent a certain number of miles or kilometers on Earth. If a map of the United States used one inch to represent a thousand miles—how wide would the United States be on the map?

Small-Scale Maps

Some maps show a large area, such as a continent, or a region. Imagine that you are in a satellite orbiting Earth. Your space ship is 100 miles above the Nile Valley. From this altitude, you can see the entire river and the surrounding river valley. Everything looks very small—like the locations on a a small-scale map. Because it covers such a large area, a small-scale map does not show many details.

From your satellite, you might notice some lights about halfway north on the Nile River. The modern city of Luxor is located on the site of the ancient Egyptian capital of Thebes. You can also find the location of Luxor on this small-scale map. This map shows the length of the Nile River in Egypt, and you can find Luxor about halfway up the Nile on the east bank of the river.

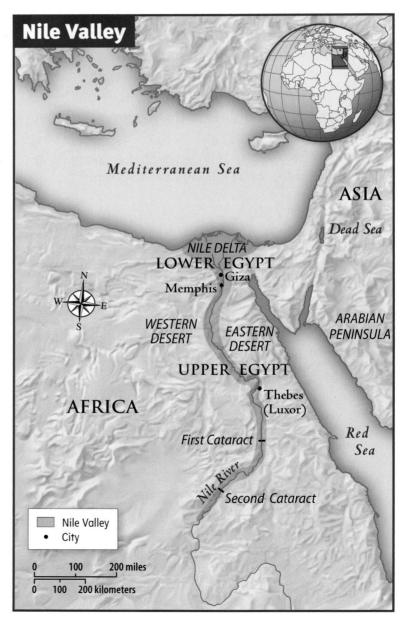

Large-Scale Maps

Now imagine that your satellite is flying only a few miles above Earth. You can see only a small area of the Nile Valley. However, you can see buildings and ancient monuments. You can also see roads and highways. This is like looking at a a large-scale map. The large-scale map shows a small area, but has more detail than a small-scale map.

The large-scale map on this page shows the streets of the modern city of Luxor. The ruins of many ancient Egyptian buildings can still be seen in Luxor. If you wanted to find the Temple of Karnak in Luxor, for example, you would use the large-scale map that shows only the city of Luxor and some of the more important buildings in the city.

Compare the scales on the two maps. What is the scale on page GH10? Is it larger or smaller than the scale on page GH11? Why do you think this is so? People choose the map that contains the information they need.

Think About It
Why might you want to have large-scale maps and small-scale maps if you are planning a trip to Egypt?

Luxor, Egypt, Today

Luxor

Nile River

Cornishe

Open Air Museum

Karnak Temple Complex

Avenue of the Sphinxes

To Airport →

Al-Karnak

Luxor

Pala Hotel

Youth Hostel

Luxor Museum

To Archaeological Sites ←

Tourist Ferry

Faluccas

Mena Palace Hotel

Station St.

Faluccas

Luxor Temple

Train Station

Tourist Ferry

Luxor Hotel

Winter Palace Hotel

N
W   E
S

| 0 | .5 | 1 mile |
| 0 | .5 | 1 kilometer |

The Americas: GDP 2006

CANADA

UNITED STATES

BAHAMAS

BELIZE
HONDURAS
NICARAGUA
PANAMA
MEXICO
VENEZUELA
GUYANA
SURINAME

CUBA
JAMAICA
HAITI
DOMINICAN
REPUBLIC

GUATEMALA
EL SALVADOR
COSTA RICA
COLOMBIA
ECUADOR
PERU
BOLIVIA
CHILE

TRINIDAD &
TOBAGO

BRAZIL

PARAGUAY
URUGUAY
ARGENTINA

Each box represents 10 billion U.S. dollars

Use a Cartogram

A cartogram is a special kind of map that helps you to compare information about countries on the map. A cartogram does not show the physical sizes of countries. It compares information about countries, such as populations or economies. A country that is geographically quite large, such as Canada, may appear small on a cartogram comparing the size of the national economies of North America.

It is important to understand that a cartogram compares information among nations. You need to read the title of a cartogram to understand what is being compared. It may be population, or economies, or how much is spent on health and welfare by each nation in the cartogram.

You will also need to bring some of your own knowledge to read a cartogram. You have to know that Canada is one of the largest countries in the world to understand that its economy is not as large as its land size.

Think About It Why might the sizes of countries get larger or smaller on different cartograms?

Time Zone Map

You may already know that people who live in different states set their clocks at different times. This happens because the Earth spins. Where the sun is shining in one area, it is dark in another. If it were the same time all over Earth, the sun would be shining in the middle of the night at some point on our planet.

This is why Earth is divided into 24 time zones. Each time zone is set to a different hour of the day. To help you figure out what time it is someplace else in the world, you would use a Time Zone Map. This kind of map shows the number of hours that any place is ahead or behind the time at the Prime Meridian.

For example, find Moscow on the map. The time in Moscow is five hours behind the time in Irkutsk. As you traveled west, you would advance the calendar date one day. As you traveled east, you would lose one day.

Think About It Why do you think the lines on the time zone map are not perfectly straight when they go across nations?

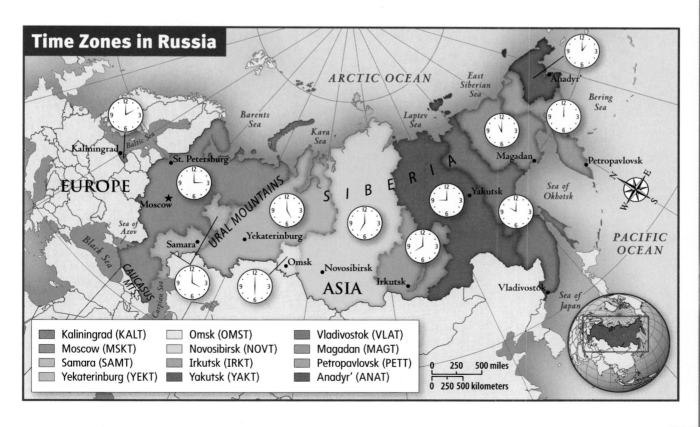

ARCTIC OCEAN

80°N

160°W   120°W   80°W   40°W

GREENLAND

Mackenzie
River

60°N   ALASKA RANGE
Mt. McKinley
20,320 ft.
(6,194 m)

Arctic Circle

NORTH
AMERICA

CANADIAN SHIELD

40°N

ROCKY MOUNTAINS

Mississippi River

APPALACHIAN MTS.

ATLANTIC
OCEAN

PACIFIC OCEAN

Tropic of Cancer

20°N

Rio
Grande

Gulf of
Mexico

Caribbean Sea

0° Equator

Amazon River

SOUTH
AMERICA

ANDES MOUNTAINS

20°S

Tropic of Capricorn

Mt. Aconcagua
22,834 ft.
(6,960 m)

ATLANTIC
OCEAN

40°S

PACIFIC OCEAN

Cape Horn

60°S

Antarctic Circle

80°W

Weddell
Sea

120°W

40°W

160°W

Vinson Massif
16,067 ft.
(4,897 m)

ARCTIC OCEAN

40°E 80°E 120°E 160°E 80°N

Lena River

Yenisey River

Ob River

60°N

Sea of Okhotsk

URAL MTS.

Volga River

EUROPE

ALPS

Mont Blanc
15,711 ft.
(4,807 m)

Caspian Sea

Black Sea ▲ Mt. Elbrus
18,510 ft.
(5,642 m)

ASIA

GOBI

40°N

Mediterranean Sea

HINDU KUSH

HIMALAYA

Yangtze River

Tropic of Cancer

SYRIAN DESERT

Ganges River

▲ Mt. Everest
29,035 ft.
(8,850 m)

20°N

SAHARA

Nile River

Red Sea

DECCAN PLATEAU

Arabian Sea

South China Sea

Philippine Sea

PACIFIC OCEAN

AFRICA

Congo River

Mt. Kilimanjaro
19,340 ft.
(5,895 m)
▲

Equator 0°

INDIAN OCEAN

NAMIB DESERT

KALAHARI DESERT

Coral Sea

Tropic of Capricorn

GREAT SANDY DESERT

20°S

AUSTRALIA

Cape of Good Hope

Darling River

Mt. Kosciuszko
7,310 ft.
(2,228 m)
▲

N
W   E
S

40°S

0   1,000   2,000 miles
0   1,000   2,000 kilometers

40°E 80°E 120°E 160°E 60°S

Antarctic Circle

80°S

ANTARCTICA

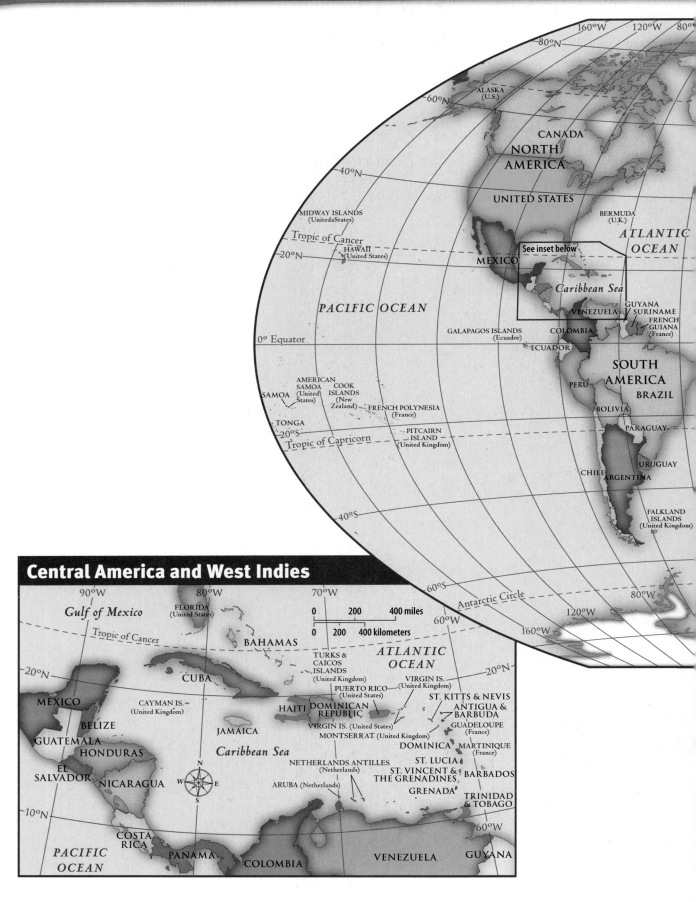

80°N

160°W   120°W   80°W

ALASKA
(U.S.)

60°N

CANADA

NORTH
AMERICA

40°N

UNITED STATES

BERMUDA
(U.K.)

ATLANTIC
OCEAN

MIDWAY ISLANDS
(UnitedaStates)

Tropic of Cancer

See inset below

HAWAII
(United States)

MEXICO

Caribbean Sea

20°N

GUYANA
VENEZUELA   SURINAME
FRENCH
GUIANA
(France)

PACIFIC OCEAN

GALAPAGOS ISLANDS
(Ecuador)

COLOMBIA

0° Equator

ECUADOR

SOUTH
AMERICA

PERU

BRAZIL

AMERICAN
SAMOA
(United
States)

COOK
ISLANDS
(New
Zealand)

SAMOA

FRENCH POLYNESIA
(France)

BOLIVIA

TONGA

PITCAIRN
ISLAND
(United Kingdom)

PARAGUAY

20°S

Tropic of Capricorn

URUGUAY

CHILE

ARGENTINA

40°S

FALKLAND
ISLANDS
(United Kingdom)

60°S

Antarctic Circle

80°W

120°W

160°W

Central America and West Indies

90°W   80°W   70°W

Gulf of Mexico

FLORIDA
(United States)

0   200   400 miles

0   200   400 kilometers

Tropic of Cancer

BAHAMAS

ATLANTIC
OCEAN

20°N

TURKS &
CAICOS
ISLANDS
(United Kingdom)

60°W

20°N

CUBA

VIRGIN IS.
(United Kingdom)

MEXICO

CAYMAN IS.
(United Kingdom)

PUERTO RICO
(United States)

ST. KITTS & NEVIS

HAITI DOMINICAN
REPUBLIC

ANTIGUA &
BARBUDA

BELIZE

GUADELOUPE
(France)

GUATEMALA

JAMAICA

VIRGIN IS. (United States)

HONDURAS

MONTSERRAT (United Kingdom)

DOMINICA MARTINIQUE
(France)

Caribbean Sea

EL
SALVADOR

NICARAGUA

NETHERLANDS ANTILLES
(Netherlands)

ST. LUCIA

ST. VINCENT &
THE GRENADINES

BARBADOS

N
W   E
S

ARUBA (Netherlands)

GRENADA

TRINIDAD
& TOBAGO

10°N

60°W

COSTA
RICA

PACIFIC
OCEAN

PANAMA

COLOMBIA

VENEZUELA

GUYANA

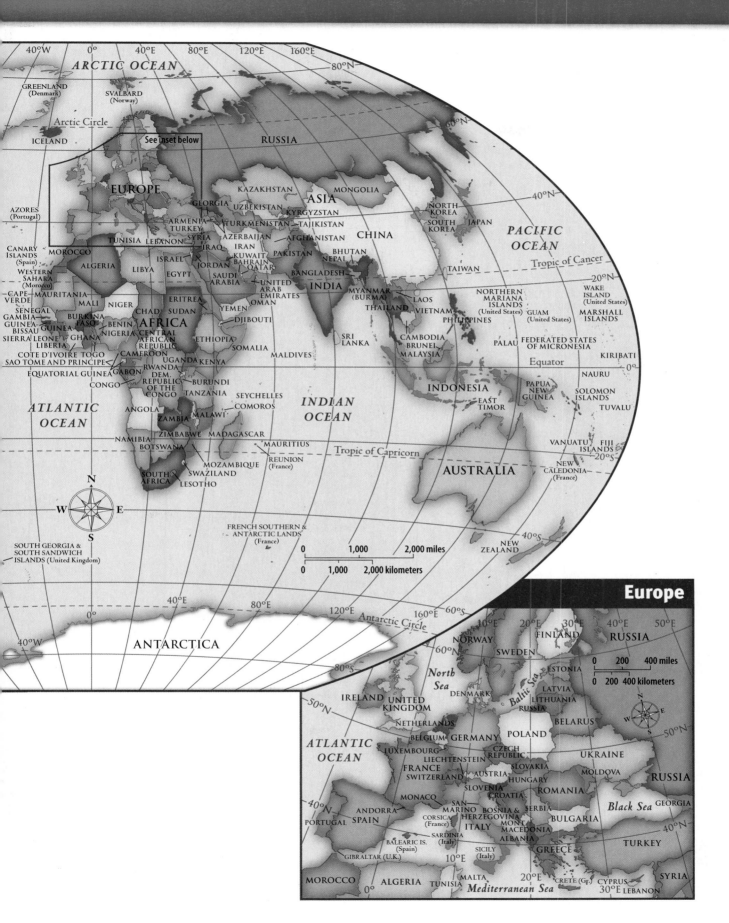

ARCTIC OCEAN

40°W 0° 40°E 80°E 120°E 160°E 80°N

GREENLAND
(Denmark)

SVALBARD
(Norway)

Arctic Circle

ICELAND

See inset below

RUSSIA

60°N

EUROPE

AZORES
(Portugal)

GEORGIA

KAZAKHSTAN

MONGOLIA

ASIA

40°N

UZBEKISTAN

ARMENIA

KYRGYZSTAN

NORTH
KOREA

TURKEY

TURKMENISTAN

TAJIKISTAN

SOUTH
KOREA

JAPAN

PACIFIC
OCEAN

CANARY
ISLANDS
(Spain)

TUNISIA

LEBANON

SYRIA

AZERBAIJAN

AFGHANISTAN

CHINA

MOROCCO

IRAQ

IRAN

ALGERIA

ISRAEL

LIBYA

EGYPT

JORDAN

KUWAIT

BAHRAIN

PAKISTAN

BHUTAN

NEPAL

Tropic of Cancer

TAIWAN

WAKE
ISLAND
(United States)

20°N

WESTERN
SAHARA
(Morocco)

QATAR

BANGLADESH

NORTHERN
MARIANA
ISLANDS
(United States)

GUAM
(United States)

CAPE
VERDE

MAURITANIA

MALI

NIGER

ERITREA

SAUDI
ARABIA

UNITED
ARAB
EMIRATES

INDIA

MYANMAR
(BURMA)

LAOS

VIETNAM

MARSHALL
ISLANDS

SENEGAL

CHAD

SUDAN

YEMEN

OMAN

THAILAND

PHILIPPINES

GAMBIA

BURKINA

BENIN

DJIBOUTI

PALAU

FEDERATED STATES
OF MICRONESIA

GUINEA-
BISSAU

GUINEA

FASO

NIGERIA

AFRICA

CENTRAL
AFRICAN
REPUBLIC

SRI
LANKA

CAMBODIA

KIRIBATI

SIERRA LEONE

LIBERIA

GHANA

ETHIOPIA

BRUNEI

MALAYSIA

COTE D'IVOIRE

TOGO

CAMEROON

UGANDA

KENYA

SOMALIA

MALDIVES

Equator

0°

SAO TOME AND PRINCIPE

EQUATORIAL GUINEA

GABON

RWANDA-

DEM.
REPUBLIC
OF THE
CONGO

BURUNDI

INDONESIA

EAST
TIMOR

PAPUA
NEW
GUINEA

NAURU

CONGO

TANZANIA

SEYCHELLES

INDIAN
OCEAN

SOLOMON
ISLANDS

TUVALU

ATLANTIC
OCEAN

ANGOLA

ZAMBIA

MALAWI

COMOROS

ZIMBABWE

MADAGASCAR

NAMIBIA

BOTSWANA

MAURITIUS

REUNION
(France)

Tropic of Capricorn

AUSTRALIA

VANUATU

FIJI
ISLANDS

20°S

NEW
CALEDONIA
(France)

MOZAMBIQUE

SWAZILAND

SOUTH
AFRICA

LESOTHO

N

W   E

S

FRENCH SOUTHERN &
ANTARCTIC LANDS
(France)

0   1,000   2,000 miles

NEW
ZEALAND

40°S

SOUTH GEORGIA &
SOUTH SANDWICH
ISLANDS (United Kingdom)

0   1,000   2,000 kilometers

40°E

80°E

120°E

160°E

60°S

40°W

0°

Antarctic Circle

ANTARCTICA

80°S

Europe

20°E

30°E

40°E

50°E

NORWAY

FINLAND

RUSSIA

60°N

SWEDEN

0   200   400 miles

North
Sea

ESTONIA

0   200   400 kilometers

IRELAND

UNITED
KINGDOM

DENMARK

Baltic Sea

LATVIA

N

LITHUANIA

W   E

RUSSIA

NETHERLANDS

S

BELGIUM

GERMANY

POLAND

BELARUS

50°N

ATLANTIC
OCEAN

LUXEMBOURG

CZECH
REPUBLIC

LIECHTENSTEIN

SLOVAKIA

UKRAINE

FRANCE

AUSTRIA

HUNGARY

SWITZERLAND

SLOVENIA

MOLDOVA

RUSSIA

MONACO

CROATIA

ROMANIA

40°N

ANDORRA

SAN
MARINO

BOSNIA &
HERZEGOVINA

SERBIA

Black Sea

GEORGIA

PORTUGAL

SPAIN

CORSICA
(France)

ITALY

MONT.

BULGARIA

40°N

SARDINIA
(Italy)

MACEDONIA

ALBANIA

TURKEY

BALEARIC IS.
(Spain)

SICILY
(Italy)

GREECE

GIBRALTAR (U.K.)

MOROCCO

ALGERIA

TUNISIA

MALTA

CRETE (Gr.)

CYPRUS

SYRIA

10°E

20°E

30°E

LEBANON

Mediterranean Sea

EUROPE

ASIA

ARCTIC OCEAN

Oodaaq Island

Lincoln Sea

Queen

Ellesmere Island

Elizabeth

Islands

HAYES PENINSULA

Greenland Sea

Gunnbjorn 12,139 ft. (3,700 m) ▲

ICELAND

Chukchi Sea

Point Barrow

Melville Island

Banks Island

Devon Island

Greenland

Bering Strait

NORTH SLOPE

Beaufort Sea

Somerset

Prince of Wales I.

Baffin Bay

Bering Sea

SEWARD PENINSULA

BROOKS RANGE

Yukon R.

Victoria Island

BOOTHIA PENINSULA

Baffin Island

Davis Strait

Cape Farewell

Mt. McKinley 20,320 ft. (6,194 m) ▲ ALASKA

ALASKA RANGE

MACKENZIE MTS.

MELVILLE PEN.

Foxe Basin

KENAI PENINSULA

YUKON PLATEAU

Mackenzie R.

Great Bear Lake

C A N A D A

Southampton Island

Hudson Strait

Ungava Bay

Labrador Sea

Mt. Logan 19,551 ft. (5,959 m) ▲

Gulf of Alaska

Great Slave Lake

Hudson Bay

ALEXANDER ARCHIPELAGO

Peace R.

Slave R.

C A N A D I A N   S H I E L D

Belcher Islands

Island of Newfoundland

Kodiak Island

Queen Charlotte Islands

COAST MOUNTAINS

Athabasca R.

Columbia Mts.

Lake Athabasca

Churchill R.

James Bay

LAURENTIAN MTS.

Gulf of St. Lawrence

AVALON PENINSULA

FRASER PLATEAU

Saskatchewan R.

Lake Winnipeg

GASPÉ PEN.

Cape Breton Island

Vancouver Island

R O C K Y

Lake Superior

St. Lawrence R.

Nova Scotia

Prince Edward Island

OLYMPIC PENINSULA

CASCADE RANGE

COLUMBIA PLATEAU

Snake R.

M O U N T A I N S

G R E A T

P L A I N S

Missouri River

Lake Michigan

Lake Huron

Ottawa ✪

Lake Ontario

Lake Erie

Gulf of Maine

Bay of Fundy

Cape Cod

Cape Mendocino

SIERRA NEVADA

Great Salt Lake

GREAT BASIN

COLORADO PLATEAU

Platte

CENTRAL LOWLAND

Long Island

ATLANTIC OCEAN

COAST RANGES

Death Valley -282 ft. (-86 m)

Mt. Whitney 14,494 ft. (4,418 m) ▲

U N I T E D   S T A T E S

Colorado R.

Arkansas River

OZARK PLATEAU

Ohio R.

APPALACHIAN MOUNTAINS

Washington, D.C. ✪

Chesapeake Bay

Bermuda (U.K.)

Channel Islands

Grand Canyon

HIGH PLAINS

Red River

Mississippi R.

C O A S T A L

Cape Hatteras

SONORAN DESERT

BAJA CALIFORNIA

Rio Grande

SIERRA MADRE OCCIDENTAL

M E X I C O

SIERRA MADRE ORIENTAL

Gulf of Mexico

P L A I N

Florida Keys

BAHAMAS

Nassau ✪

Tropic of Cancer

DOMINICAN REPUBLIC

PACIFIC OCEAN

Gulf of California

Tropic of Cancer

Havana ✪

CUBA

W E S T   I N D I E S

Hispaniola

HAITI

Virgin Islands Guadeloupe

Orizaba 18,855 ft. (5,747 m) ▲

Cozumel Island

Cayman Islands (U.K.)

Port-au-Prince ✪

Santo Domingo ✪

Martinique

Puerto Rico (U.S.)

México City ✪

YUCATÁN PENINSULA

Kingston ✪

JAMAICA

TRINIDAD & TOBAGO

GUATEMALA

BELIZE

Belmopan ✪

Isthmus of Tehuantepec

Caribbean Sea

Port-of-Spain ✪

Guatemala City ✪

HONDURAS

San Salvador ✪

Tegucigalpa ✪

NICARAGUA

EL SALVADOR

Managua ✪

Lake Nicaragua

COSTA RICA

San José ✪

Isthmus of Panamá

PANAMA

Panamá ✪

SOUTH AMERICA

CENTRAL AMERICA

— International boundary

✪ National capital

▲ Mountain peak

| 0 | 300 | 600 miles |

| 0 | 300 | 600 kilometers |

N W E S

Equator

SOUTH AMERICA: POLITICAL/PHYSICAL

NORTH AMERICA

ISTHMUS OF PANAMA

Caribbean Sea

ATLANTIC OCEAN

N
W E
S

Maracaibo
Caracas
VENEZUELA
Orinoco R.
GUIANA HIGHLANDS
Georgetown
GUYANA
Paramaribo
SURINAME
Cayenne
FRENCH GUIANA (France)

Bogotá
Cali
COLOMBIA

Negro River

Equator   Equator

Quito
ECUADOR
Guayaquil

Galápagos Islands (Ecuador)

0°   0°

Amazon River

AMAZON BASIN

River

Tapajós River
Xingú River

PERU

ANDES MOUNTAINS

Lima

Madeira River

Tocantins River

São Francisco River

BRAZIL

Lake Titicaca

Arequipa
La Paz
BOLIVIA
Santa Cruz
Sucre

Brasília
BRAZILIAN
HIGHLANDS
River

15°S   15°S

ATACAMA DESERT

Paraguay R.

PARAGUAY

Paraná

Mt. Ojos del Salado
22,572 ft.
(6,880 m)

Asunción

São Paulo
Rio de Janeiro

Tropic of Capricorn   Tropic of Capricorn

CHILE

Paraná River

Mt. Aconcagua
22,834 ft. (6,960 m)
Valparaíso
Santiago

Rosario

Salto
URUGUAY
Montevideo

PACIFIC OCEAN

ARGENTINA

Buenos Aires
Rio de la Plata

30°S   30°S

Concepción

PAMPAS

PATAGONIA

ATLANTIC OCEAN

Falkland Islands (Islas Malvinas) (U.K.)

| 0 | 250 | 500 miles |
| 0 | 250 | 500 kilometers |

45°S   45°S

Strait of Magellan

TIERRA DEL FUEGO

South Georgia (U.K.)

Cape Horn

Legend:
— International boundary
⊛ National capital
• Other city
▲ Mountain peak

105°W   90°W   75°W   60°W   45°W   30°W

15°N
15°N

GH19

ASIA: POLITICAL/PHYSICAL

PACIFIC OCEAN

ARCTIC OCEAN

EUROPE

AFRICA

INDIAN OCEAN

Bering Strait

Bering Sea

East Siberian Sea

Wrangel Island

New Siberian Islands

Laptev Sea

Kara Sea

CHUKCHI RANGE

KOLYMA RANGE

KAMCHATKA PENINSULA

Sea of Okhotsk

Kuril Islands

Sakhalin

SIKHOTE ALIN MTS.

Amur River

CHERSKIY MTS.

VERKHOYANSK MTS.

STANOVOY MTS.

YABLONOVYY MTS.

TAYMYR PENINSULA

CENTRAL SIBERIAN PLATEAU

Lena River

Angara River

Lake Baikal

Yenisey River

RUSSIA

WEST SIBERIAN PLAIN

Ob River

Irtysh River

YAMAL PEN.

URAL MOUNTAINS

Arctic Circle

Moscow

Ural River

Sea of Azov

Black Sea

Bosporus

Mediterranean Sea

Caspian Sea

Lake Balkhash

KAZAKHSTAN

Astana

Bishkek

KYRGYZSTAN

Tashkent

UZBEKISTAN

TURKMENISTAN

Ashgabat

Baku

AZERBAIJAN

GEORGIA

Tbilisi

Yerevan

ARMENIA

TURKEY

Ankara

CYPRUS

Nicosia

Beirut

LEBANON

Damascus

SYRIA

ISRAEL

Jerusalem

Amman

JORDAN

Baghdad

IRAQ

Kuwait

KUWAIT

SAUDI ARABIA

Riyadh

Manama

BAHRAIN

Doha

QATAR

Abu Dhabi

UNITED ARAB EMIRATES

Muscat

OMAN

Sanaa

YEMEN

Gulf of Aden

Socotra

Red Sea

IRAN

Tehran

IRANIAN PLATEAU

AFGHANISTAN

Kabul

Dushanbe

TAJIKISTAN

Islamabad

PAKISTAN

New Delhi

INDIA

INDIAN SUBCONTINENT

NEPAL

Kathmandu

HIMALAYA

Mt. Everest 29,035 ft. (8,850 m)

Thimphu

BHUTAN

BANGLADESH

Dhaka

MYANMAR (BURMA)

Yangon (Rangoon)

Naypyidaw

LAOS

Vientiane

THAILAND

Bangkok

CAMBODIA

Phnom Penh

VIETNAM

Hanoi

Hainan

Andaman Sea

Andaman Islands (India)

Nicobar Islands (India)

Bay of Bengal

SRI LANKA

Colombo

MALDIVES

Male

Maldive Islands (India)

Laccadive Islands (India)

Chagos Archipelago (British Indian Ocean Territory)

Arabian Sea

WESTERN GHATS

EASTERN GHATS

Godavari River

Yangtze River

CHINA

Beijing

NORTH CHINA PLAIN

Yellow River

Chang Jiang River

QINLING MTS.

KUNLUN MTS.

ALTUN SHAN

TAKLIMAKAN

TARIM BASIN

Turpan Depression

GOBI

MONGOLIA

Ulaanbaatar

NORTH KOREA

Pyongyang

SOUTH KOREA

Seoul

Yellow Sea

East China Sea

Taiwan

JAPAN

Tokyo

Sea of Japan

Hokkaido

Honshu

Shikoku

Kyushu

Philippine Sea

PHILIPPINES

Manila

South China Sea

MALAYSIA

Kuala Lumpur

Singapore

BRUNEI

Bandar Seri Begawan

Borneo

Sumatra

Java Sea

Celebes Sea

Sulawesi

Java

Jakarta

INDONESIA

EAST TIMOR

Dili

Arafura Sea

New Guinea

Equator

Tropic of Cancer

Legend

— International boundary

▲ Mountain peak

⊛ National capital

1,000 miles

500   1,000 kilometers

GH20

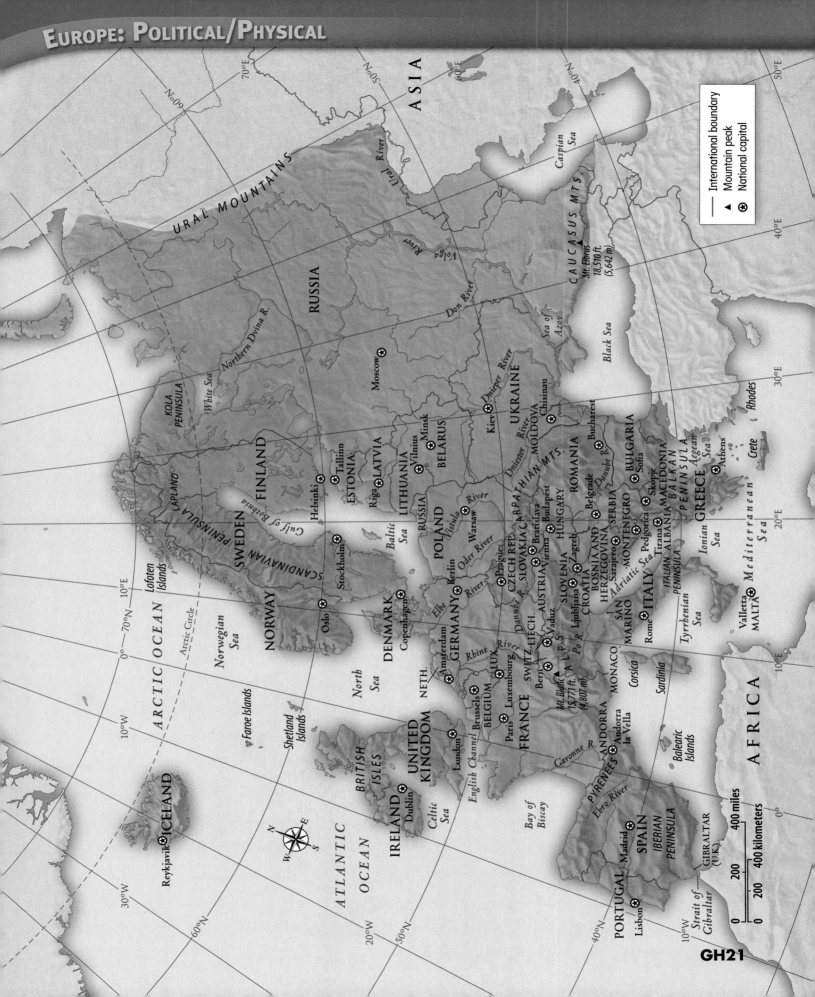

Legend

— International boundary
▲ Mountain peak
⊛ National capital

ASIA

URAL MOUNTAINS

Ural River

Caspian Sea

RUSSIA

Volga River

Don River

CAUCASUS MTS.

Mt. Elbrus 18,510 ft. (5,642 m)

Northern Dvina R.

White Sea

KOLA PENINSULA

Sea of Azov

Black Sea

Moscow ⊛

Dnieper River

UKRAINE

Chisinau ⊛

Rhodes

FINLAND

Dniester River

MOLDOVA

Bucharest ⊛

Crete

Aegean Sea

Tallinn ⊛

ESTONIA

LATVIA

Riga ⊛

Minsk ⊛

BELARUS

Kiev ⊛

CARPATHIAN MTS.

ROMANIA

Danube R.

BULGARIA

Sofia ⊛

BALKAN PENINSULA

GREECE

Athens ⊛

LAPLAND

SCANDINAVIAN PENINSULA

Helsinki ⊛

Gulf of Bothnia

Baltic Sea

RUSSIA

Vilnius ⊛

LITHUANIA

Vistula River

Warsaw ⊛

POLAND

CZECH REP.

Prague ⊛

SLOVAKIA

Bratislava ⊛

Budapest ⊛

HUNGARY

Belgrade ⊛

SERBIA

Skopje ⊛

MACEDONIA

ALBANIA

Tirana ⊛

Mediterranean Sea

SWEDEN

Stockholm ⊛

Oder River

Berlin ⊛

Elbe

GERMANY

Oder River

AUSTRIA

Vienna ⊛

SLOVENIA

Ljubljana ⊛

Zagreb ⊛

CROATIA

BOSNIA AND HERZEGOVINA

Sarajevo ⊛

MONTENEGRO

Podgorica ⊛

Adriatic Sea

ITALY

Ionian Sea

Valletta ⊛ MALTA

NORWAY

Oslo ⊛

DENMARK

Copenhagen ⊛

NETH.

Amsterdam ⊛

Rhine River

LUX.

SWITZ.

LIECH.

Vaduz ⊛

Bern ⊛

Po R.

SAN MARINO

Rome ⊛

MONACO

Corsica

Tyrrhenian Sea

Sardinia

ITALIAN PENINSULA

ARCTIC OCEAN

Norwegian Sea

Arctic Circle

Faroe Islands

Lofoten Islands

Shetland Islands

North Sea

BRITISH ISLES

UNITED KINGDOM

London ⊛

Brussels ⊛

BELGIUM

Paris ⊛

FRANCE

Mt. Blanc 15,771 ft. (4,807 m)

ANDORRA

Andorra la Vella ⊛

PYRENEES

Garonne R.

Balearic Islands

AFRICA

ATLANTIC OCEAN

ICELAND

Reykjavik ⊛

IRELAND

Dublin ⊛

Celtic Sea

English Channel

Bay of Biscay

Ebro River

SPAIN

Madrid ⊛

IBERIAN PENINSULA

GIBRALTAR (U.K.)

PORTUGAL

Lisbon ⊛

Strait of Gibraltar

Scale

400 miles
400 kilometers
0 200 400
0 200 400

N E S W

GH21

International boundary
National capital ⊗
Other city •

1,000 miles
500
0
1,000 kilometers
500
0
500

N E S W (compass rose)

NORTH PACIFIC OCEAN

SOUTH PACIFIC OCEAN

INDIAN OCEAN

Equator

Tropic of Cancer

Tropic of Capricorn

International Date Line

15°N
0°
15°S
30°S
45°S
15°N
Tropic of Cancer

135°W
150°W
165°W
180°
165°E
150°E
135°E
120°E

Hawaiian Islands (U.S.)

Pitcairn Islands (U.K.)

French Polynesia (France)

Cook Islands (N.Z.)

KIRIBATI

Tokelau Islands (N.Z.)
SAMOA
American Samoa (U.S.)
Apia
Niue (N.Z.)
TONGA
Nukuʻalofa

Wake Island (U.S.)

MARSHALL ISLANDS
Majuro
Tarawa

Wallis & Futuna (France)
TUVALU
Funafuti
FIJI ISLANDS
Suva

NAURU
SOLOMON ISLANDS
Honiara

VANUATU
Port-Vila
New Caledonia (France)

Northern Mariana Islands (U.S.)

Guam (U.S.)

Caroline Islands
FEDERATED STATES OF MICRONESIA
Palikir

PALAU
Melekeok

Philippine Sea

Timor Sea

Arafura Sea
Darwin
ARNHEM LAND
KIMBERLEY PLATEAU
GREAT SANDY DESERT
GIBSON DESERT
GREAT VICTORIA DESERT
BARKLY TABLELAND
SIMPSON DESERT
Lake Eyre
GREAT ARTESIAN BASIN

AUSTRALIA

NULLARBOR PLAIN
Great Australian Bight
Perth
DARLING RANGE
Adelaide

PAPUA NEW GUINEA
Port Moresby

CAPE YORK PENINSULA
Coral Sea
Great Barrier Reef
GREAT DIVIDING RANGE

Brisbane
Sydney
Canberra
Melbourne
Hobart
Bass Strait
Tasmania

Darling R.
Murray R.

Tasman Sea

NEW ZEALAND
Auckland
Wellington
Christchurch
Cook Strait
Dunedin
Stewart Island

Equator

Tropic of Capricorn

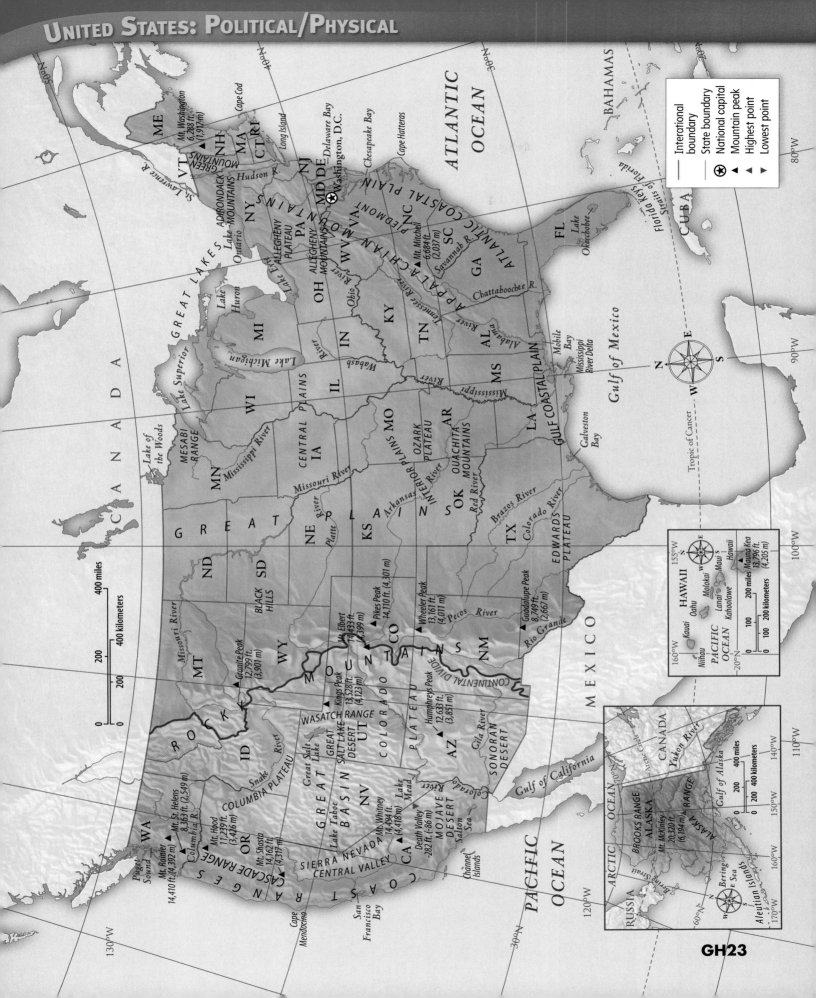

Legend:
- International boundary
- State boundary
- ⊛ National capital
- ◄ Mountain peak
- ◄ Highest point
- ► Lowest point

ATLANTIC OCEAN

PACIFIC OCEAN

CANADA

MEXICO

Gulf of Mexico

BAHAMAS

CUBA

States: ME, NH, VT, MA, CT, RI, NY, NJ, MD, DE, PA, OH, WV, VA, NC, SC, GA, FL, KY, TN, AL, MS, LA, AR, MO, IA, MN, WI, MI, IN, IL, ND, SD, NE, KS, OK, TX, NM, CO, WY, MT, ID, UT, NV, AZ, CA, OR, WA

Physical features:
- Mt. Washington 6,288 ft. (1,917 m)
- Cape Cod
- Long Island
- Delaware Bay
- Chesapeake Bay
- Cape Hatteras
- ADIRONDACK MOUNTAINS
- GREEN MOUNTAINS
- St. Lawrence R.
- Hudson R.
- Lake Ontario
- Lake Erie
- Lake Huron
- Lake Superior
- Lake Michigan
- GREAT LAKES
- ALLEGHENY PLATEAU
- ALLEGHENY MOUNTAINS
- APPALACHIAN MOUNTAINS
- PIEDMONT
- ATLANTIC COASTAL PLAIN
- Mt. Mitchell 6,684 ft. (2,037 m)
- Savannah R.
- Chattahoochee R.
- Ohio River
- Wabash River
- Tennessee River
- Alabama River
- Mobile Bay
- GULF COASTAL PLAIN
- Mississippi River Delta
- Lake Okeechobee
- Florida Keys
- Straits of Florida
- CENTRAL PLAINS
- Mississippi River
- Missouri River
- OZARK PLATEAU
- OUACHITA MOUNTAINS
- INTERIOR PLAINS
- Arkansas River
- Red River
- Brazos River
- Colorado River
- Galveston Bay
- EDWARDS PLATEAU
- MESABI RANGE
- Lake of the Woods
- Platte River
- GREAT PLAINS
- BLACK HILLS
- Pikes Peak 14,110 ft. (4,301 m)
- Wheeler Peak 13,161 ft. (4,011 m)
- Pecos River
- Rio Grande
- Guadalupe Peak 8,749 ft. (2,667 m)
- Granite Peak 12,799 ft. (3,901 m)
- Mt. Elbert 14,433 ft. (4,399 m)
- ROCKY MOUNTAINS
- Kings Peak 13,528 ft. (4,123 m)
- CONTINENTAL DIVIDE
- Humphreys Peak 12,633 ft. (3,851 m)
- COLORADO PLATEAU
- Gila River
- SONORAN DESERT
- Gulf of California
- WASATCH RANGE
- GREAT SALT LAKE DESERT
- Great Salt Lake
- GREAT BASIN
- Lake Tahoe
- Lake Mead
- MOJAVE DESERT
- Salton Sea
- Death Valley -282 ft. (-86 m)
- Mt. Whitney 14,494 ft. (4,418 m)
- SIERRA NEVADA
- CENTRAL VALLEY
- COLUMBIA PLATEAU
- Snake River
- Columbia R.
- Mt. St. Helens 8,363 ft. (2,549 m)
- Mt. Hood 11,239 ft. (3,426 m)
- Mt. Shasta 14,162 ft. (4,317 m)
- CASCADE RANGE
- COAST RANGES
- Mt. Rainier 14,410 ft. (4,392 m)
- Puget Sound
- Cape Mendocino
- San Francisco Bay
- Channel Islands
- Missouri River

Compass rose: N, E, S, W

Scale:
- 400 miles
- 400 kilometers
- 200, 0

Tropic of Cancer

HAWAII inset:
- Kauai
- Niihau
- Oahu
- Molokai
- Lanai
- Maui
- Kahoolawe
- Hawaii
- Mauna Kea 13,796 ft. (4,205 m)
- PACIFIC OCEAN
- 200 miles
- 200 kilometers
- 100
- 155°W, 160°W, 20°N

ALASKA inset:
- CANADA
- RUSSIA
- Yukon River
- BROOKS RANGE
- ALASKA RANGE
- Mt. McKinley 20,320 ft. (6,194 m)
- Gulf of Alaska
- ARCTIC OCEAN
- Arctic Circle
- Bering Strait
- Bering Sea
- Aleutian Islands
- PACIFIC OCEAN
- 400 miles
- 400 kilometers
- 200, 100
- 70°N, 60°N
- 140°W, 150°W, 160°W, 170°W

Longitude lines: 130°W, 120°W, 110°W, 100°W, 90°W, 80°W, 70°W

GH23

EUROPE

ASIA

ATLANTIC OCEAN

Madeira Islands (Portugal)

Strait of Gibraltar

Algiers · Tunis

Rabat

MOROCCO

Canary Islands (Spain)

Mediterranean Sea

Gulf of Gabes

Gulf of Sidra

Tripoli

NILE DELTA

SINAI PENINSULA

Suez Canal

Cairo

WESTERN SAHARA (Morocco)

Cape Blanc

MAURITANIA

Nouakchott

ALGERIA

LIBYA

EGYPT

Nile R.

Tropic of Cancer

S A H A R A

ATLAS MOUNTAINS

AHAGGAR MOUNTAINS

TIBESTI MOUNTAINS

LIBYAN DESERT

Lake Nasser

NUBIAN DESERT

Red Sea

AIR RANGE

MALI

Niger

Senegal R.

Dakar · SENEGAL

Banjul

GAMBIA

Bamako

BURKINA FASO

Niamey

River

NIGER

CHAD

Lake Chad

N'Djamena

SUDAN

Khartoum

Atbara R.

Blue Nile R.

ERITREA

Asmara

DJIBOUTI

Gulf of Aden

Djibouti

SOMALI PENINSULA

Bissau

GUINEA-BISSAU

GUINEA

Conakry

SIERRA LEONE

Freetown

Monrovia

LIBERIA

Ouagadougou

BENIN

NIGERIA

Abuja

COTE GHANA D'IVOIRE

Yamoussoukro

TOGO

Accra

Lome

Porto-Novo

Cape Palmas

Gulf of Guinea

Malabo

EQUATORIAL GUINEA

SAO TOME AND PRINCIPE

Sao Tome

Cape Lopez

Benue River

CENTRAL AFRICAN REPUBLIC

Bangui

CAMEROON

Yaounde

Libreville

GABON

Brazzaville

CONGO

Ubangi R.

Congo R.

CONGO BASIN

Lomami R.

Kasai R.

White Nile R.

ETHIOPIAN HIGHLANDS

Addis Ababa

ETHIOPIA

SUDD

Lake Albert

Lake Turkana

UGANDA

Kampala

SOMALIA

Mogadishu

GREAT RIFT VALLEY

Lake Victoria

Kigali

RWANDA

Bujumbura

BURUNDI

KENYA

Nairobi

Mt. Kilimanjaro ▲ 19,340 ft. (5,895 m)

INDIAN OCEAN

Pemba Island

Dodoma

Zanzibar Island

Dar es Salaam

TANZANIA

SEYCHELLES

Lake Tanganyika

Cape Delgado

Equator

ATLANTIC OCEAN

CABINDA (Angola)

Kinshasa

Luanda

Kwango R.

DEMOCRATIC REPUBLIC OF THE CONGO

BIE PLATEAU

ANGOLA

Cubango R.

Cuando R.

NAMIBIA

Windhoek

NAMIB DESERT

KALAHARI DESERT

Okavango BASIN

ZAMBIA

Lake Kariba

Lusaka

Zambezi R.

Harare

ZIMBABWE

Victoria Falls

MALAWI

Lilongwe

Lake Malawi

Moroni

COMOROS

Mayotte (France)

Mozambique Channel

MOZAMBIQUE

MADAGASCAR

Antananarivo

Limpopo R.

BOTSWANA

Gaborone

Pretoria

Maputo

SWAZILAND

Mbabane

Vaal R.

Maseru

LESOTHO

Bloemfontein

Orange River

DRAKENSBERG

SOUTH AFRICA

Cape Town

Cape of Good Hope

Cape Agulhas

Tropic of Capricorn

N
W · E
S

Legend

- ✪ National capital
- —— International boundary
- ----- Disputed boundary
- ▲ Mountain peak
- ≡ Waterfall

0 · 500 · 1,000 miles
0 · 500 · 1,000 kilometers

40°N · 30°N · 20°N · 10°N · 0° · 10°S · 20°S · 30°S · 40°S

20°W · 10°W · 0° · 10°E · 20°E · 30°E · 40°E · 50°E

Glossary

This glossary will help you to pronounce and understand the meanings of the vocabulary terms in this book. The page number at the end of the definition tells you where the word first appears.

PRONUNCIATION KEY

a	at	ē	me	ō	old	ū	use	ng	song
ā	ape	i	it	ô	fork	ü	rule	th	thin
ä	far	ī	ice	oi	oil	ù	pull	th	this
âr	care	î	pierce	ou	out	ûr	turn	zh	measure
e	end	o	hot	u	up	hw	white	ə	about, taken, pencil, lemon, circus

A

abacus (ab'ə kəs) a frame with sliding beads, used for mathematical solutions (p. 202)

adobe (ə dō'bē) clay and straw formed into sun-dried bricks (p. 113)

agriculture (ag'ri kul chər) the ways of growing crops and raising animals (p. 25)

alliance (ə lī'əns) an agreement to work together (p. 277)

ancestor (an'ses tər) a family member who lived a long time ago (p. 7)

annul (ə nəl') to legally undo (p. 199)

anthropologist (an thrə pol'ə jist) a scientist who studies human culture (p. 7)

anti-Semitism (an tē sem'i tizm) the hatred of Jews (p. 311)

apartheid (ə pär'tīd) a legal structure supporting racial segregation in South Africa (p. 315)

aqueduct (ak'wə dukt) a bridge-like structure that carries water to cities (p. 104)

archaeologist (är kē ol'ə jist) a scientist who studies the remains of human culture (p. 7)

archipelago (är kə pel'ə gō) a cluster of many islands (p. 321)

armistice (är'mə stis) an agreement to stop fighting (p. 279)

arms race (ärmz rās) the competition to design and build the most powerful weapons (p. 304)

artifact (är'ti fakt) anything made and used by people in the past (p. 22)

artisan (är'tə zən) a skilled worker (p. 57)

astrolabe (as'trə lāb) an instrument used for navigating by the stars (p. 146)

astronomy (as tron'ə mē) the study of stars and planets (p. 38)

B

bar graph (bär graf) a graph that shows information using rectangles at different lengths (p. 153)

barter (bär′tər) to trade goods and services in payment, rather than to pay with cash or coins (p. 25)

Bastille (ba stēl′) a royal prison in Paris, France, which was attacked on July 14, 1789, beginning the French Revolution (p. 251)

bazaar (bə zär′) a market place with rows of shops and tents (p. 144)

boycott (boi′kot) a form of organized protest in which people refuse to do business with a company or nation (p. 250)

caliph (ka′lif) a Muslim political and religious leader in the years following the death of Muhammad (p. 141)

caravan (kar′a van) a group of traveling traders (p. 135)

caravel (kar′a vel) a cargo ship designed for ocean travel in the 1400s (p. 235)

caste (kast) a social group in Hinduism into which a person is born (p. 56)

cathedral (ka thē′drəl) a large Christian church led by a bishop (p. 187)

causeway (kôz′wā) raised roadway used for travel across water (p. 120)

census (sen′səs) a count of every person living in a country (p. 104)

century (sen′chə rē) one hundred years (p. 23)

circa (sûr′kə) around or about a certain date (p. 23)

circumnavigate (sûr kum nav′ə gāt) to sail completely around Earth (p. 237)

city-state (si′ tē stāt) a city and its nearby land and villages (p. 32)

civil disobedience (siv′əl dis ō bē′dē əns) to peacefully protest by refusing to obey laws that are felt to be unjust (p. 307)

civil service (siv′əl sûr′vis) the structure which employs people to work for a government (p. 74)

civil war (siv′əl wär) a war between groups within a country (p. 100)

climate (klī′mit) a place's weather over a long period of time (p. 2)

climograph (klī′mō graf) a graph that gives information about the weather of a place over a period of time (p. 233)

code (kōd) a collection of laws (p. 35)

codex (kō′ deks) a long book written by the Maya (p. 117)

Cold War (kōld wär) the global struggle for power between the United States and the Soviet Union (p. 303)

command economy (kə mand i kon′ ə mē) an economy completely controlled and directed by a government (p. 283)

commune (kom′ ūn) a community where labor, resources, and property are shared (p. 296)

communism (kom′ ūn izm) a political system in which government controls all land and industry (p. 281)

complex (kom′ pleks) a cluster of buildings (p. 219)

concentration camps (kon sen trā′shun kamps) prisons where Nazis enslaved and murdered millions of people (p. 286)

confederation (kon fed ə rā′ shun) an alliance of states or provinces, such as the Confederation of Canada (p. 256)

conquistador (kon kēs′ tə dôr) a Spanish conqueror of Native Americans (p. 242)

consul (kon′ səl) an elected leader of ancient Rome (p. 98)

consumer (kon sü′ mər) one who buys goods and uses services (p. 10)

contour (kon′ tür) imaginary lines that enclose areas of equal elevation on a topgraphic map (p. 45)

convent (kon′ vent) a building housing a community of nuns (p. 187)

coup (kü) a sudden overthrow of the government(p. 321)

covenant (kuv′ə nənt) an agreement or promise (p. 36)

Crusade (krü′sād) war for control of the holy land (p. 188)

cultural region (kul′chûr əl rē′jən) an area in which a culture is expressed (p. 6)

Cultural Revolution (kul′chûr əl rev ō lü′shun) the destruction of China's cultural past during the rule of Mao Zedong (p. 297)

D

daimyo (dīm′yō) a military and political leader in feudal Japan (p. 212)

decade (dek′ād) a ten-year time span (p. 23)

deity (dē′i tē) a god or a goddess (p. 56)

demand (də mand′) the desire or need for goods or services (p. 162) see **supply**

democracy (də mok′rə sə) a form of government in which citizens participate and hold ultimate power (p. 91)

depression (di presh′ ən) an era of high unemployment and economic hardship (p. 285)

dhow (dou) an Arabian boat with a large triangular sail (p. 171)

diffusion (di fü′shun) the spreading of one thing into another (p. 9)

divan (di von′) a council of advisors in the Ottoman Empire (p. 150)

divine right (di vīn′ rīt) the belief that monarchs receive the right to rule from God and that they need answer only to God (p. 249)

domesticate (də mest′ik āt) to adapt and raise wild plants and animals for agricultural needs (p. 26)

double bar graph (dub′əl bär graf) a graph that compares information with parallel rectangles (p. 101)

dynasty (dī′nə stē) a family that rules for several generations (p. 42)

E

elevation (el ə vā′shun) the height of land above sea level (p. 45)

empire (em′pīr) several territories and nations ruled by one authority (p. 32)

Enlightenment (en līt′ən ment) an era of scientific and ethical progress in Europe during the 1600s and 1700s (p. 232)

environment (en vīr′ən ment) the surroundings in which people, plants, and animals live (p. 21)

epic (ep′ik) a long poem that tells about the life of a hero (p. 62)

export (eks pôrt) a trade good which is sent to another country (p. 62) see **import**

F

factory (fak′tə rē) a building where goods are manufactured (p. 259)

fascist (fash′ist) someone who supports a political movement that combines nationalism and racism and demands total government control (p. 285)

feudalism (fü′dəl izm) political and economic system based on loyalty to a lord (p. 182)

flow chart (flō chärt) a chart that uses pictures or words to show, step by step, how something is done (p. 205)

Forbidden City (fôr bid′ən si tē) the walled complex of palaces and temples where the Chinese emperor and his court lived (p. 203)

G

genocide (jen ō sīd) the planned destruction of an ethnic, political, or cultural group (p. 289)

geocentric (jē ō sen′ trik) the idea that Earth is the center of the universe (p. 229) see **heliocentric**

geography (jē og′rə fē) the study of Earth's surface (p. 2)

global economy (glō′bəl i kon′ə mē) the flow of goods, services, and currency among nations (p. 327)

globalization (glō′bəl i zā′shun) the policy of connecting nations through trade, politics, culture, and technology (p. 327)

glyph (glif) a picture symbol (p. 117)

GMT abbreviation for Greenwich Mean Time, the line of longitude where each day begins. (page 239) see **Greenwich Mean Time**

granary (grā nə rē) where grains are stored (p. 169)

Grand Mufti (grand məf′tē) the highest religious official of Sunni Islam (p. 150)

Grand Vizier (grand vi zēr′) an advisor to the Ottoman sultan (p. 150)

Great Leap Forward (grāt lēp fôr′wärd) Chairman Mao's failed attempt to modernize China's economy in the 1950s (p. 296)

Green Revolution (grēn re və lü′shun) a movement to increase agricultural production in India and other countries in the 1960s (p. 308)

Greenwich Mean Time or GMT (gren′ ich mēn tīm) the starting point for counting hours across the world's time zones, located in Greenwich, England (p. 239)

griot (grē′ō) a west African storyteller and keeper of oral histories (p. 164) see **oral history**

gross domestic product (grōs′ də mes′tik prod′ əkt) the value of all the goods and services in one nation (p. 11)

guerrilla (gə ril′ə) an armed person who uses sabotage and surprise attacks against a government or an invading military force (p. 322)

guild (gild) an organized group of artisans in the same industry or trade during the Middle Ages in Europe (p. 183)

H

harbor (här′bər) a sheltered place along a coast (p. 85)

heliocentric (hē lē ō sen′ trik) a sun-centered description of the universe (p. 229) see **geocentric**

hieroglyphics (hī′ər ə glif′iks) an ancient Egyptian writing system that used picture symbols (p. 44)

historical map (his tôr′i kəl map) a map that shows places and events of the past (p. 95)

humanism (hū′ mən izm) a philosophy based in human values and achievement (p. 193)

hunter-gatherer (hun′tər gath′ ər ər) one who hunted animals and gathered wild plants for food (p. 21)

hydroponics (hī drō pon′ iks) method of growing crops in water used widely in the Inca Empire (p. 124)

I

immunity (i mūn′i tē) resistance to a disease (p. 243)

imperialism (im pîr′ē əl izm) claiming colonies to increase a nation's wealth and power (p. 263)

import (im pôrt) a trade good that is brought into one country from another country (p. 62) see **export**

Industrial Revolution (in dəs′trē əl rev ō lü′shun) a period starting in the 1700s when goods began to be made by machines (p. 259)

inflation (in flā′ shun) period when prices shoot upward (p. 105)

infusion (in fū shun) the introduction of one substance, idea, or influence into another (p. 9)

innovation (in ō vā′shun) a new idea, or way of doing something (p. 9)

Inquisition (in kwə zi′shun) a church-run court (p. 197)

irrigation (îr ə gā shun) a system of transporting water from a river, lake, or well to make farming possible in dry region (p. 30)

J

Janissaries (jan ə sâ rē) elite Turkish soldiers of the Ottoman Empire (p. 150)

L

line graph (līn graf) a diagram that presents patterns and amounts of change over a period of time (p. 153)

loess (les) a rich yellow soil of the Huang He valley in China (p. 65)

M

manor (man′ər) an area of land controlled by a lord during the Middle Ages in Europe (p. 182)

manufacturing economy (man yə fak chər ing i kon ə mē) an economy based on production of goods (p. 12)

martial law (mär′shəl lô) temporary military rule over a population (p. 323)

mestizo (mes tē zō) a person of mixed Spanish and Native American ancestry (p. 254)

Middle Passage (mid′əl pas′ij) the distance captured Africans were shipped across the Atlantic Ocean to the West Indies (p. 246)

minaret (min ə ret′) a tower from which Muslims are called to pray (p. 145)

mint (mint) to make coins or other currency (p. 161)

Mogul (mü gəl) a Persian, Mongolian, or Turkish Muslim who lived in India (p. 207)

monarchy (mon′ər kē) a government led or directed by a king or queen (p. 91)

monastery (mon′ə ste rē) a building housing a group of monks (p. 187)

monotheism (mon ə thē′ iz əm) belief in one God (p. 36)

monsoon (mon sün′) strong wind over the Arabian Sea that changes direction, causing a wet season and a dry season over India (p. 53)

mosque (mosk) a Muslim place of worship (p. 145)

mummy (mu′mē′) a dead body that has been prepared for preservation, especially in Egypt (p. 49)

Muslim (muz′lim) one who follows Islam (p. 136)

N

nationalism (nash' ə nə liz əm) loyalty to one's country (p. 263)

NATO (nā' tō) a military alliance formed in 1949 between nations in North America and Europe to oppose communism (p. 302)

Northwest Passage (nôrth west pas' ij) a water route believed by explorers of the 1500s and 1600s to cross North America between the Atlantic and Pacific Oceans (p. 238)

O

oasis (ō ā'sis) a place in a desert where water can be found (p. 133)

Old Stone Age (ōld stōn āj) the earliest period of human existence before humans learned to make objects out of any metal (p. 21)

oligarchy (o'li gär kē) government based on the rule of the wealthy and powerful (p. 91)

oracle (ôr' ə kəl) a priest believed to be able to predict the future (p. 67)

oral history (ôr'əl his' tə rē) stories told aloud and passed from one generation to the next (p. 7)

P

papyrus (pə pī'rəs) an Egyptian reed that was used to make a kind of paper (p. 44)

parallel time line (par'ə lel tīm'līn) a diagram of events arranged in time order for two different regions or people's lives (p. 23)

patrician (pə tri' shən) member of Rome's powerful families (p. 98)

Pax Romana (pox rō ma' nə) a period of peace under the Roman Empire between 27 B.C. and A.D. 180 (p. 103)

pharaoh (fâr' ō) all-powerful king in ancient Egypt (p. 42)

philosopher (fə los'ə fər) someone who seeks truth and the right way to live (p. 89)

physical region (fiz'i kəl rē'jən) a land region that shares a natural environment (p. 2)

pictograph (pik'tə graf) a graph that uses a picture that stands for an object or idea (p. 67)

picture graph (pik chər graf) a graph in which pictures or symbols represent a certain amount of something (p. 291)

pilgrimage (pil' grə mij) a journey to a holy place or shrine (p. 137)

plague (plāg) a disease or event that causes suffering for many people (p. 93)

plebeian (pli bē' ən) poor farmer or shopkeeper of ancient Rome (p. 98)

polytheism (pol ē thē'iz əm) belief in many gods (p. 32)

porcelain (pôr'sə lin) a special clay that can be shaped and baked to make dishes and vases (p. 202)

producer (prə dü' sər) those who provide services or make goods (p. 10)

projection (prə jek'shən) the method of transferring the information from a globe onto a flat surface (p. 221)

propaganda (prop ə gand' ə) spreading ideas to influence opinion (p. 285)

pueblo (pweb'lō) a Spanish name for a Southwest culture (p. 112)

pyramid (pîr'ə mid) a massive stone building with a square base and four triangular sides, used as a tomb in ancient Egypt (p. 50)

Q

quipu (kē' pü) colored and knotted strings used by the Inca to send messages (p. 125).

R

raja (rä jə) a prince or other ruler of India (p. 59)

Reformation (re′fər mā′ shən) a movement that established the Christian Protestant churches in Europe (p. 198)

refugee (ref ′yū jē′) someone who flees from home to avoid death or suffering (p. 316)

reincarnation (rē in cär nā′shən) the cycle of rebirth (p. 56)

Renaissance (ren′ə säns) a period of cultural growth in Europe in the 1500s (p. 193)

republic (ri pub′lik) a government in which the leader is voted into office (p. 98)

resource distribution map (rē′sôrs dis tri bū′shən map) a map that shows where natural resources are located in a nation or region (p. 169)

S

samurai (sam′ü rī) an elite warrior of feudal Japan (p. 212)

sanction (sangk′shən) an economic, legal, or military penalty applied against one nation by another nation or group of nations (p. 315)

scribe (skrīb) a person whose job was to write or copy documents, records, and other documents in ancient times (p. 33)

serf (sûrf) a servant who farmed the land (p. 182)

service economy (sûr′vis i kon′ə mē) an economy based on providing services (p. 12)

shah (sha) the title of a Persian or Iranian monarch (p. 208)

sharia (sha rē′ə) Islamic laws that govern personal and public life (p. 312)

Shinto (shin′tō) the nature-based religion of Japan (p. 211)

shogun (shō′ gən) the head of an army or military government (p. 211)

shogunate (shō′ gən ət) the period when shoguns ruled Japan between ca. 800 and 1867 (p. 212)

sickle (si′kəl) a tool with a curved blade that is used to cut grain and tall grass (p. 158)

Silk Road (silk rōd) a network of trade routes across Asia stretching from China to the Mediterranean Sea (p. 75)

space race (spās rās) the challenge among world governments to explore outer space and reach the moon (p. 304)

specialize (spesh′ə līz) train to do one particular kind of work (p. 25)

sphere of influence (sfirs ov in′ flū əns) an area of China that Europeans took from the Chinese government and ruled by European laws (p. 266)

standardization (stan dər dəz ā′ shən) the process of making things similar (p. 71)

strait (strāt) a narrow waterway that connects larger bodies of water (p. 217)

strike (strīk) to protest working conditions by refusing to work in the factory until workers' demands are met (p. 261)

sultan (sul′ tən) the monarch of a Muslim country, especially the Ottoman Empire (p. 149)

supply (sə plī′) the amount of goods or services available at any time (p. 162) see **demand**

surplus (sûr′ pləs) an extra amount of food, money, or other goods beyond what is needed for personal use (p. 25)

T

technology (tek nol′ə jē) tools and methods used to help humans perform tasks (p. 21)

terrace (ter′is) flat area dug out of hillsides (p. 122)

terrorist (ter′ ər ist) one who uses fear and violence to achieve political goals (p. 312)

textile (teks′tīl) cloth made from woven threads (p. 159)

theory (thē′ə rē) an explanation about how or why something happens (p. 229)

time line (tīm līn) a diagram of events arranged in the order in which they took place (p. 23)

time zone (tīm zōn) any of 24 divisions of the Earth's surface that standardizes the local time (p. 239)

topographic map (top ə graf′ik) a physical map that shows features of Earth's surface (p. 45)

totalitarian (tō tal i târ′ ē ə niz əm) government or dictator that has almost total control over people's lives (p. 283)

totem (tō′təm) an animal symbol of a group or family (p. 113)

Triangular Trade (trī ang′gyə lər trād) the trade route between Africa, the West Indies, and North America (p. 246)

tsunami (tsü nä′mē) a tidal wave caused by an undersea earthquake (p. 86)

tyrant (tī′rənt) one who rules harshly and with absolute power (p. 91)

union (ūn′yən) a group of workers who unite to improve working conditions (p. 261)

vaccine (vak sēn′) a method of preventing diseases, such as smallpox (p. 232)

values (val′ūz) principles or standards of what people consider to be important in life (p. 8)

vassal (vas′əl) one who swore loyalty to a lord (p. 182)

W

warlord (wôr lôrd) a military leader with his own army (p. 66)

Warsaw Pact (wôr sô pakt) an alliance between the Soviet Union and Eastern European communist countries organized to oppose NATO (p. 302)

Wat (wot) a Buddhist temple and school (p. 219)

Index

This index lists many topics that appear in the book, along with the pages on which they are found. Page numbers after a *c* refer you to a chart or diagram, after a *g*, to a graph, after an *m*, to a map, after a *p*, to a photograph or picture, and after a *q*, to a quotation.

D

Index

Index

Illustration Credits: 12-13: Paul Mirocha. 19: (tl) Gary Overacre. 26-27: Inklink. 30-31: Richard Hook. 32: Gary Overacre. 44: Inklink. 47: Gary Overacre. 49: Inklink. 50-51: Richard Hook. 54-55: Richard Hook. 131: (tl) Steve Chorney. 226: (tr) Steve Chorney. 236: Roger Stewart. 252: Marc Sott. 291: John Kurtz.

Photo Credits: All Photographs are by Macmillan/McGraw-Hill (MMH) except as noted below.

1: Kaushik Sengupta/AP Photos. 2-3: (bkgd) Stan Osolinski/Getty Images. 3: (b) Dallas and John Heaton/Free Agents Limited/CORBIS. 3: (t) Ken Welsh/Alamy Images. 4: (b) Arnulf Husmo/Getty Images; (t) Ladislav Janicek/zefa/CORBIS. 4-5: (b) Peter Lik/Panoramic Images. 5: (b) Pablo Corral V/CORBIS; (t) David Muench/Getty Images. 6: (c) O. Louis Mazzatenta/National Geographic Image Collection. 6-7: (b) Peter Bowater/Alamy Images. 7: (t) Christy Gavitt/Woodfin Camp & Associates. 8: (b) Peter Sanders/HAGA/The Image Works, Inc. 8-9: (b) Orion Press/Getty Images. 9: (c) Misha Japaridze/AP Photos; (t) Karan Kapoor/Getty Images. 10: (bl) Yadid Levy/Robert Harding Picture Library. 10-11: (b) Panoramic Image/Robert Harding Picture Library. 11: (t) Bohemian Nomad Picturemakers/CORBIS. 14: (b) Peter Bowater/Alamy Images. 16: (b) Mina Chapman/CORBIS/PunchStock; (t) Blend Images Photography/PunchStock. 17: Dinodia Photo Library. 18: (bl) Kenneth Garrett/National Geographic Image Collection; (br) Gavin Hellier/Getty Images; (tl) Photo Archives of the South Tyrol Museum of Archaeology/South Tyrol Museum of Archaeology, Italy; (tr) Erich Lessing/Art Resource, NY. 19: (bl) Borromeo/Art Resource, NY; (br) Keren Su/China Span/Alamy Images; (tr) The British Library/Art Archive. 20: (bc) Centre for Development Studies, University of Bergen, Norway/Blombos Cave Project; (bl) National Anthropological Museum Mexico/Dagli Orti/Art Archive; (br) Centre for Development Studies, University of Bergen, Norway/Blombos Cave Project. 20-21: Larry Dale Gordon/Getty Images. 21: (b) National Anthropological Museum Mexico/Dagli Orti/Art Archive. 22: (b) Larry Dale Gordon/Getty Images; (tl) Centre for Development Studies, University of Bergen, Norway./Blombos Cave Project; (tr) Centre for Development Studies, University of Bergen, Norway/Blombos Cave Project. 24: (bl) Ric Ergenbright/CORBIS. 24-25: Ric Ergenbright/CORBIS. 25: (bl) Erich Lessing/Art Resource, NY; (br) Siede Preis/Getty Images. 26: (b) David Butow/CORBIS SABA. 27: (c) Ric Ergenbright/CORBIS. 28: (br) The Granger Collection, New York. 28-29: Nik Wheeler/CORBIS. 32-33: (b) The Granger Collection, New York. 33: (r) Nik Wheeler/CORBIS; (tl) The Granger Collection, New York. 34: (bc) Topham/The Image Works, Inc.; (bl) Erich Lessing/Art Resource, NY; (br) Erich Lessing/Art Resource, NY. 34-35: Oriental Institute, University of Chicago. 35: (c) Erich Lessing/Art Resource, NY. 36: (b) Alan & Sandy Carey/Getty Images. 37: (b) Topham/The Image Works, Inc.; (t) Erich Lessing/Art Resource, NY. 38: Robert Harding Picture Library Ltd/Alamy Images. 39: (b) Alan & Sandy Carey/Getty Images; (t) Erich Lessing/Art Resource, NY. 40: (bc) J Marshall - Tribaleye Images/Alamy Images. 40-41: Chad Ehlers/Alamy Images. 42: (bl) Archivo Iconografico, S.A./CORBIS; (br) Musée du Louvre Paris/Dagli Orti/Art Archive. 42-43: (b) Jim Henderson/Alamy Images. 43: (bc) Aegyptisches Museum, SMPK, Berlin/Boltin Picture Library/Bridgeman Art Library; (bl) Erich Lessing/Art Resource, NY; (br) J Marshall - Tribaleye Images/Alamy Images; (t) Luxor Museum, Egypt/Dagli Orti/Art Archive. 44: (c) Chad Ehlers/Alamy Images. 46: (bc) HIP/Art Resource, NY; (br) David Sutherland/Getty Images. 46-47: Kenneth Garrett. 48: (bl) HIP/Art Resource, NY; (r) Ann Ronan Picture Library/HIP/The Image Works, Inc.; (tl) Electa/akg-images. 48-49: (bkgd) akg-images. 49: (bl) Egyptian National Museum, Cairo, Egypt/Bridgeman Art Library; (tl) HIP/Art Resource, NY. 50: (bl) David Sutherland/Getty Images. 51: (cr) HIP/Art Resource, NY; (t) Egyptian Museum Cairo/Dagli Orti (A)/Art Archive. 52: (br) Victoria & Albert Museum, London/Art Resource, NY. 52-53: Dilip Mehta/Woodfin Camp & Associates. 54: (t) Randy Olson/National Geographic Image Collection. 55: (tl) CORBIS; (tr) CORBIS. 56: (b) Dinodia Photo Library; (br) Victoria & Albert Museum, London/Art Resource, NY. 57: (bl) Historical Picture Archive/CORBIS; (br) Historical Picture Archive/CORBIS. 58: (bc) davies & starr/Getty Images; (bl) Art Archive; (br) Werner Forman/Art Resource, NY. 58-59: Chris Lisle/CORBIS. 59: (b) Art Archive. 60: (bl) davies & starr/Getty Images. 61: (c) Masahiko Sato/Getty Images; (t) David Hanson/Getty Images. 62: Werner Forman/Art Resource, NY. 63: (bl) Marc Bernheim/Woodfin Camp & Associates; (br) David Hanson/Getty Images. 64: (bc) Beijing Institute of Archaeology/Laurie Platt Winfrey/Art Archive; (bl) Library of Congress, Geography and Map Division. 64-65: Gina Corrigan/Robert Harding Picture Library. 65: Library of Congress, Geography and Map Division. 67: (b) British Museum, London, UK/Bridgeman Art Library; (t) Beijing Institute of Archaeology/Laurie Platt Winfrey/Art Archive. 68: Asian Art & Archaeology, Inc./CORBIS. 69: (c) Gina Corrigan/Robert Harding Picture Library; (tl) Dorling Kindersley Ltd. Picture Library. 70: (bcl) The Granger Collection, New York; (bcr) Snark/Art Resource, NY; (bl) ChinaStock; (br) Science Museum/Science & Society Picture Library. 70-71: Lee White/CORBIS. 71: (b) ChinaStock. 72: (b) The Granger Collection, New York; (t) Burstein Collection/CORBIS. 73: Bibliothèque Nationale Paris/Art Archive. 74: Snark/Art Resource, NY. 75: (r) Réunion des Musées Nationaux/Art Resource, NY. 76: Getty Images. 77: (b) Lee White/CORBIS; (tl) Science Museum/Science & Society Picture Library;

(tr) Science Museum/Science & Society Picture Library. 78: (c) National Anthropological Museum Mexico/Dagli Orti/Art Archive. 80: (b) Peter Adams/Getty Images; (t) Amos Morgan/Getty Images. 81: Steve Vidler/SuperStock. 82: (bl) Robert Harding Picture Library Ltd./Alamy Images; (br) Cosmo Condina/Alamy Images; (tl) Araldo de Luca/CORBIS; (tr) Musée Lapidaire d'Art Paien Arles/Dagli Orti/Art Archive. 83: (bl) Robert Frerck/Odyssey Productions, Chicago; (br) Jeremy Horner/Getty Images; (tl) Dagli Orti/Art Archive; (tr) New-York Historical Society, New York, USA/Bridgeman Art Library. 84: (bc) Giraudon/Bridgeman Art Library; (bl) Roy Rainford/Getty Images; (br) SuperStock. 84-85: Roy Rainford/Getty Images. 85: (b) Peter Connolly/akg-images. 86: (b) Freeman Patterson/Masterfile; (c) Private Collection Paris/Dagli Orti/Art Archive. 87: (bkgd) Arthur S. Aubry/Getty Images; (border) Wetzel & Company; (tc) Giraudon/Bridgeman Art Library; (tl) Archivo Iconografico, S.A./CORBIS; (tr) Bridgeman Art Library. 88: (bkgd) Phidias/CORBIS; (r) Scala/Art Resource, NY; (1st Row L to R) National Archaeological Museum, Athens, Greece/Bridgeman Art Library; Museo Nazionale Palazzo Altemps Rome/Dagli Orti/Art Archive; (2nd Row L to R) Museum of Fine Arts, Boston, Massachusetts, USA/Bridgeman Art Library; Erich Lessing/Art Resource, NY; Scala/Art Resource, NY. (3rd Row L to R) Erich Lessing/Art Resource, NY; Erich Lessing/Art Resource, NY; Christie's Images/SuperStock; (4th Row L to R) Musée du Louvre Paris/Dagli Orti/Art Archive; Dagli Orti/Art Archive; Ancient Art & Architecture Collection, Ltd. 89: (c) Private Collection, Paris/Dagli Orti/Art Archive. 89: (t) SuperStock. 90: (bc) Peter Connolly/akg-images; (bl) Peter Connolly/akg-images; (br) Museo Nazionale Taranto/Dagli Orti/Art Archive. 90-91: Peter Connolly/akg-images. 92: (bl) Peter Connolly/akg-images; (br) Peter Connolly/akg-images. 92-93: (bkgd) Stapleton Collection/CORBIS. 94: (bl) Museo Nazionale Taranto/Dagli Orti/Art Archive; (br) Peter Connolly/akg-images. 96: (bc) Scala/Art Resource, NY; (bl) Art Wolfe/Getty Images; (br) Museo della Civilta Romana Rome/Dagli Orti/Art Archive. 96-97: Greg Stott/Masterfile. 97: (b) Art Wolfe/Getty Images. 98: Scala/Art Resource, NY. 99: Scala/Art Resource, NY. 100: (l) Museo della Civilta Romana Rome/Dagli Orti/Art Archive; (r) Scala/Art Resource, NY 101: Peter Connolly/akg-images. 102: (bcl) akg-images; (bcr) Scala/Art Resource, NY; (bl) Galleria d'Arte Moderna Rome/Dagli Orti (A)/Art Archive; (br) Historical Picture Archive/CORBIS. 102-103: Galleria d'Arte Moderna Rome/Dagli Orti (A)/Art Archive. 103: (bkgd) David Wasserman/Jupiterimages/PunchStock; (c) akg-images. 105: (b) David McNew/Hulton Archive/Getty Images; (t) akg-images. 106: (r) Erich Lessing/Art Resource, NY. 106-107: (bkgd) Flat Earth. 107: (bkgd) Flat Earth; (c) Scala/Art Resource, NY. 108-109: (b) Historical Picture Archive/CORBIS. 109: (c) akg-images. 110: (bcl) Joseph Froelich Collection/Ohio Historical Society; (bcr) SuperStock; (bl) Kevin Fleming/CORBIS; (br) Palenque Site Museum Chiapas/Dagli Orti/Art Archive. 110-111: Kevin Fleming/CORBIS. 112: Tony Linck/SuperStock. 113: (bc) Werner Forman/Art Resource, NY; (bkgd) Arthur S. Aubry/Getty Images; (bl) Werner Forman/Art Resource, NY; (br) Joseph Froelich Collection/Ohio Historical Society. 114: (b) SuperStock. 115: Danny Lehman/CORBIS. 116: Scott Barrow, Inc./SuperStock. 117: (c) Danny Lehman/CORBIS; (t) Palenque Site Museum Chiapas/Dagli Orti/Art Archive. 118: (bcl) H Rogers/Art Directors & TRIP Photo Library; (bcr) Jeremy Horner/CORBIS; (bl) Steve Vidler/SuperStock; (br) Getty Images. 118-119: Steve Vidler/SuperStock. 119: (b) Museo Regional de Antropologia Merida Mexico/Dagli Orti/Art Archive. 120: (bl) H Rogers/Art Directors & TRIP Photo Library. 120-121: (b) Alison Wright/The Image Works, Inc. 122-123: (b) Jeremy Horner/CORBIS. 123: (t) Pedro de Osma Museum Lima/Mireille Vautier/Art Archive. 124: (b) Getty Images. 125: (c) Alison Wright/The Image Works, Inc.; (t) Werner Forman/CORBIS.; (tl) Loren McIntyre/Woodfin Camp & Associates; (tr) Werner Forman/Art Resource, NY. 126: Peter Connolly/akg-images. 128: (b) Freeman Patterson/Masterfile; (c) Getty Images; (t) Thomas Northcut/Getty Images. 129: Patrick Ben Luke Syder/Lonely Planet Images. 130: (bl) Jonathan Blair/CORBIS; (br) Nik Wheeler/CORBIS; (tl) The Granger Collection, New York; (tr) The Granger Collection, New York. 131: (bl) SuperStock; (br) Murat Taner/zefa/CORBIS; (tr) The Granger Collection, New York. 132: (bcl) P. Hawkins/Robert Harding Picture Library; (bcr) Nabeel Turner/Getty Images; (bl) blickwinkel/Alamy Images; (br) AP Photos. 132-133: blickwinkel/Alamy Images. 134-135: (b) P. Hawkins/Robert Harding Picture Library. 135: (b) Jeffrey L. Rotman/CORBIS. 136: (c) Nabeel Turner/Getty Images. 136-137: (b) Brand X Pictures/Jupiterimages; (t) Brand X Pictures/Jupiterimages. 137: (c) Bernard O'Kane/Alamy Images. 138: (b) The Trustees of the Chester Beatty Library, Dublin/Bridgeman Art Library. 139: (b) P. Hawkins/Robert Harding Picture Library; (t) AP Photos. 140: (bcl) University Library Istanbul/Dagli Orti/Art Archive; (bcr) The Art Archive/CORBIS; (bl) Robert Frerck/Getty Images; (br) Scala/Art Resource, NY. 140-141: Robert Frerck/Getty Images. 141: (b) Adastra/Getty Images. 142: (b) University Library Istanbul/Dagli Orti/Art Archive. 143: Bridgeman Art Library. 144: (l) Charles & Josette Lenars/CORBIS. 144-145: (b) The Art Archive/CORBIS. 145: (r) Charles & Josette Lenars/CORBIS; (t) SuperStock. 146: (b) Archives Charmet/Bridgeman Art Library; (t) Scala/Art Resource, NY. 147: (r) The Art Archive/CORBIS. 148: (bc) The Granger Collection, New York; (bl) The Granger Collection, New York; (br) Robert Frerck/Odyssey Productions, Chicago. 148-149: Fergus O'Brien/Getty Images. 149: (r) The Granger Collection, New York. 150: The Granger Collection, New York. 151: (b) Topkapi Museum Istanbul/Dagli Orti/Art Archive. 152: (b)

& Co. KG/Alamy Images. 292-293: Getty Images. 293: (b) Getty Images. 294: (b) Bettmann/CORBIS. 295: William Sewell/Art Archive. 296: SV-Bilderdienst/The Image Works, Inc. 297: (b) 2005 Roger-Viollet/The Image Works, Inc.; (c) Macduff Everton/CORBIS. 298: (b) vario images GmbH & Co.KG/Alamy Images; (c) William Sewell/Art Archive. 300: (bc) AP Photos; (bl) Public Record Office/Topham-HIP/The Image Works, Inc.; (br) Getty Images. 300-301: Public Record Office/Topham-HIP/The Image Works, Inc. 302: (b) AP Photos; (t) CORBIS. 303: Gert Schütz/akg-images. 304: (b) Department of Defense; (tc) Getty Images; (tr) AP Photos. 305: (c) AP Photos; (t) Time Life Pictures/Getty Images. 306: (bl) Dagli Orti (A)/Art Archive; (br) Tom Bible/Alamy Images. 306-307: Dagli Orti (A)/Art Archive. 307: (b) Getty Images. 309: (c) Dagli Orti (A)/Art Archive; (inset) Tom Bible/Alamy Images; (t) Dinodia Photo Library. 310: (bl) Patrick Robert/Sygma/CORBIS; (br) Marco Di Lauro/Getty Images. 310-311: David Hume Kennerly/Getty Images. 311: (b) Patrick Robert/Sygma/CORBIS. 313: (b) Marco Di Lauro/Getty Images; (t) David Hume Kennerly/Getty Images. 314: (bc) EPA/CORBIS;
(bl) Paul Almasy/CORBIS; (br) Issouf Sanogo/AFP/Getty Images. 314-315: Paul Almasy/CORBIS. 315: (b) Collart Herve/CORBIS Sygma. 316: EPA/CORBIS. 318: (b) Issouf Sanogo/AFP/Getty Images; (c) Bettmann/CORBIS. 319: (b) Paul Almasy/CORBIS; (t) Mandel Ngan/AFP/Getty Images. 320: (bc) Tibor Bognar/Alamy Images; (bl) Dita Alangkara/AP Photos; (br) Morton Beebe/CORBIS. 320-321: Dita Alangkara/AP Photos. 321: (b) Choo Youn-Kong/AFP/Getty Images. 322: Tibor Bognar/CORBIS. 323: (b) Steven Mc Curry/Magnum Photos; (t) Bettmann/CORBIS. 324: (b) Morton Beebe/CORBIS. 324-325: (bkgd) Frank Chmura/Panoramic Images. 325: (c) Dita Alangkara/AP Photos; (t) Charles Lenars/CORBIS. 326: (bcl) Yann Arthus-Bertrand/CORBIS; (bcr) Jean-Marc Giboux/Getty Images; (bl) David Frazier/Getty Images; (br) Paula Bronstein/Getty Images. 326-327: CP, Fred Chartrand/AP Photos. 327: (b) Lee Foster/Bruce Coleman Inc. 328: (b) Paul A. Souders/CORBIS; (inset) Yann Arthus-Bertrand/CORBIS. 329: (b) Paul A. Souders/CORBIS; (t) James Nachtwey/VI/AP Photos. 330: (tl) Grant Neuenburg/Reuters/CORBIS; (tr) Center for Disease Control. 331: Jean-Marc Giboux/Getty Images. 332: Spencer Platt/Getty Images. 333: (b) Jean-Marc Giboux/Getty Images; (c) Paula Bronstein/Getty Images; (tl) Paula Bronstein/Getty Images; (tr) Bob Daemmrich/The Image Works, Inc. 334: (c) Time Life Pictures/Getty Images. 336: (cr) Issouf Sanogo/AFP/Getty Images; (t) Amos Morgan/Getty Images. R3: Larry Dale Gordon/Getty Images. R5: Peter Connolly/akg-images. R7: With respect to 1989.281.98 Egyptian, Ram's Head Amulet, ca. 770-657 B.C.E; Dynasty 25; late Dynastic period, gold; 1 5/8 x 1 3/8 in. (4.2 x 3.6 cm): The Metropolitan Museum of Art, Gift of Norbert Schimmel Trust, 1989 . (1989.281.98) Photograph © 1992 The Metropolitan Museum of Art. R9: Private Collection/Bridgeman Art Library. R11: Giraudon/Bridgeman Art Library. R13: Franklin D. Roosevelt Library. GH2-GH3: (t) Daryl Benson/Masterfile. GH4: (b) John Warden/Getty Images; (c) CORBIS. GH5: (b) Getty Images; (c) Ken Gillham/Robert Harding Picture Library; (t) Frans Lemmens/Getty Images.

ACKNOWLEDGMENTS

Grateful acknowledgment is given to the following authors and publishers. Every effort has been made to trace the ownership of all copyrighted material and to secure the necessary permissions to reprint these selections. In the case of some selections for which acknowledgment is not given, extensive research has failed to locate the copyright holders.